GOLF
PRO
FOR
GOD

The Lord is my strength and song,
and he is become my salvation.

—Exodus 15:2

GOLF PRO

by

with

foreword by

FOR GOD

johnny spence

oscar fraley

billy graham

centaur house/inc.
New York City
Distributed by Hawthorn Books, Inc.

Foreword

I have heard Johnny Spence's testimony and I think that everyone should
hear it.

"Therefore if any man be in Christ, he
is a new creature: old things are
passed away; behold, all things are become new." II Corinthians 5:17

Billy Graham

Illustrations

Contents

GOLF
PRO
FOR
GOD

1

I walk through the valley of the shadow of
death . . . *Psalms 23:4*

A Short Putt from Death

Shadows blurred the corners of the coffin-sized room
in the psychiatric section of the hospital in Columbia,
South Carolina. Iron bars laced their rigid fingers across
the only window. I could vaguely see the head of the
guard who was watching me through the unbreakable
glass peephole.

I knew I was only a short putt from death. On this
morning I had attempted suicide. I was an alcoholic, a
drug addict, a bum, a haggard bag of skin and bones
for whom there was no hope.

The door opened and, squinting up, I made out the white-clad forms of a nurse and a doctor. They seemed to float toward me and I felt as if I were watching from a great distance, feeling nothing, as they administered glucose intravenously into a bony arm on which the skin hung in loose folds. It came as a surprise when I realized that the arm was actually mine; I found it almost impossible to focus with my one good eye.

My other eye was useless. It had been torn out by another addict in a rest home brawl. I couldn't move even if I had wanted to, but lay there in a powerless stupor. Not just because I had lost a lung in an automobile accident through drunken driving, but also because I hadn't eaten anything in weeks. Another reason was that my hands were shackled to the sides of the bed.

The doctor's voice sounded hollow, as if it had echoed through a long corridor. "That's all we can do for him. I think you'd better call his family and then call the chaplain. I don't think he's going to make it."

The doctor, I realized far back in my clouded mind, was talking about me. Me, Johnny Spence, who had once been the youngest Class A golf professional in the country; a man who had earned a fortune, who knew just about every celebrity anyone could name, and who was accepted by all as a hail fellow and the life of endless parties.

Both of them apparently thought I was in a coma, for the doctor's voice burst forth in booming frustration. "Nurse, why is it that with all our vast resources, all our technical and medical knowledge, here is a man who wants to die and we can't save him? Why?"

There was a moment's silence before the nurse replied. "I don't know, Doctor. But it seems that when they get here in this condition, all we can do is pass them along to the morgue. It's a good thing the morgue was enlarged recently."

The thick door closed behind them, and I wished fervently that I would die. Hammers pounded mercilessly inside my head, my mouth was tinder-dry, and flames seared the walls of my stomach. Pain lanced in waves through my whole tormented body, and from somewhere deep in my own personal hell I found the strength to damn them both for not giving me another needle in my arm, a skeletal thing which already looked like my mother's old, worn-out pincushion.

How long I lay there alone I had no way of knowing. Then I heard the door open again, and two men entered. One was a white-coated guard. The other was an elderly man carrying a Bible, and I realized he must be the chaplain.

The last thing I wanted was to talk to him, so I clamped my eyelids tight as if I were asleep. But I could feel him standing over me, and my eyelids fluttered when his voice came down to me.

"Mr. Spence, I was just passing your room and thought I'd come in and have a word with you, perhaps a prayer, if you don't mind."

Who does he think he's kidding? I wondered. I knew he wasn't just passing, because this was the last room at the end of the hall and you couldn't pass it. As with me, there was no place else to go from here.

I shook my head weakly and, in a voice which was a mere whisper, said as emphatically as I could, "Nothing doing. Get away from me."

"I want to pray for you," he insisted patiently.

"No! Don't waste your time praying for me."

"Oh, yes," he pleaded. "Let's pray to God to help you."

Anger flared briefly inside of me, but my shout was a barely audible croak. "There's no such thing as God. If there is one, he turned his back on me a long time ago. So leave me alone and get the hell out of here."

"Please," he insisted, and I felt a tiny spark of shame for having talked to him in such a manner. Besides, even that minor outburst had left me limp.

"Please," he said again.

"All right," I agreed wearily, "if you want to, go ahead. But it won't do any good. I'm not worth it, mister, so don't even dirty your trousers."

His voice was gentle, but firm. "Yes, you are worth it."

Then he sank to his knees, grasped my hand firmly, and began to pray. The voice was deep and resonant, yet it was as if he were speaking to someone else in the room. "Father in heaven, I want you to come into this man's heart and give him a spark of desire to live. Let him know, God, that you never turn your back on anyone. This man thinks that he is bad. He isn't bad. I am bad, Father, I am a sinner. And if you would save me, Father, I know you'll save him."

That startled me even in the shape I was in. I had never heard a preacher refer to himself as a sinner. I had never heard a man like this talk about how bad he was. He was actually comparing himself to me. It wasn't possible for anyone to be as bad as I was, and yet here he was saying that he was—and with undoubtable sincerity.

A gimmick, that's what it was. In my business we were always looking for a gimmick to sell something or to get across an idea. What's his gimmick? I wondered. What's he trying to do—sell me on something?

But as his voice rolled on, his honesty gradually impressed itself on me. I found myself more and more fascinated by what he was saying. It was too late, of course. I knew that. There was no doubt in my mind that I was dying and beyond recall. Yet I saw the truth as he closed his prayer by saying, "Father, I want to thank you in Jesus' name."

Then, his grip tightening even more on my scrawny hand, he told me, "You're going to be all right."

There were tears on my cheeks, and my voice was hardly audible. He leaned down, with his ear close to my lips, and I asked him, "Chaplain, is it true that a drowning man sees his whole life reflected as if in a mirror? That he can see his whole life flash past?"

"I believe it is possible, Mr. Spence. "

"Well, Chaplain," I whispered, "mine just all came back to me and I want to talk about it. Do you have the time to listen?"

His grip tightened again on my arm. "Of course. I have all night if it will help you."

The guard left the room and returned within a few moments with a chair. The chaplain pulled it close to the bed on which I lay strapped and, sitting down, bent over so that once again his ear was close to my lips.

"Tell me about it, my son."

I told him, in a halting, croaking whisper, about how my parents had separated when I was fourteen years old, and how I had left school to caddy and had become a golf professional at seventeen. Then came the Sunday, after returning from church with my mother, when the club president told me I would have to be around the club all day on Sunday and, if I weren't, they would get someone else for the job. I had called my mother and told her, and she had urged me to give up the job. I refused.

"Chaplain," I said huskily, "that day I hung up the phone on my mother, I hung up the phone on God. Then came the day when the young people I associated with called me a sissy because I wouldn't drink or smoke. Being chained to this bed is my payment for traveling the road of conformity."

There were tears in the chaplain's eyes now.

"I made as much as four thousand dollars a week," I went on. "Now I've abandoned my wife and I'm dying without a cent to my name. I tried, Chaplain, to free myself from these evils. I joined alcoholic groups and entered rest homes. I visited psychiatrists. I spent more than eleven thousand dollars in one rest home. But nobody told me I was a sinner. They simply told me I was either an alcoholic or an addict. When I couldn't pay, when the money ran out, they put me out in the street, still an alcoholic and now a drug addict on top of it all. They had used the needle to try to cure me from the whiskey!"

I couldn't speak any more. My strength was about gone and I closed my eyes and lay there silently.

The chaplain's hand tightened on my arm once more. "Look to God, Johnny," he said. "Try to pray, and I'll pray for you." His voice choked and he left the room.

How long I lay there, I can't tell. But then I heard someone moving and, focusing my good eye, saw that it was the guard. He had been in the room all the time. He sounded almost ashamed.

"Mr. Spence, I was almost under your bed listening to you. But I want to tell you one thing. I know a lot of people who think Christian people are crazy. I know. I get a lot of persecution right around here in the hospital because I try to tell them.

"Look, Mr. Spence," he added, "I'm going to try to help you. I'm going to take off those manacles and let you try to move around the room."

Swiftly he freed my hands and detached the glucose clip from my foot. But then, when he started to help me get up, I pushed him away.

"Don't hurt your hands on me," I told him. "Either I do it myself or it's no good. Son, I've tried just about everything a man can put into a needle or a bottle. I've been to doctors. I've spent thousands and thousands of dollars. I've tried everything that a man can do, so don't touch me."

There was a deep hurt in his tone. "I was only trying to help you."

"I know, and I thank you. But no man can help me. I've got to do this myself."

Slowly I dragged myself erect, and from where I was able to muster the strength I'll never know. Then, unsteadily, I took three tottering steps to the barred window and clutched the casement to hold myself erect. Looking out the window, I saw lights on the street and stars twinkling in the sky, and I wondered why such simple things I'd hardly ever noticed before looked so beautiful to me at this moment.

"Son," I said to the guard, "I've never prayed out loud. But tonight I'm going to say something."

The guard sat in the chair vacated by the chaplain. "Go ahead, Mr. Spence. Get it off your chest."

I looked out into the night once again and somehow my voice became stronger. "Oh God," I prayed, "if there is a God. Tonight I know I'm going to die. I can feel it. I know what's going on. I know I've been a burden and society won't have me. There's nothing left for me but death. But before I die, do one thing for me if you will. If you're God, and you're just, and you're good as the preacher said you were, will you do this for me? My mother will be coming out here. She's the only one who hasn't forsaken me. If you'll just clean me up enough so that I won't shake and won't cry when she gets here . . . well, whatever time I have left I'll stick to you. But I want to tell my mother I've been cleaned out. I don't want any more whiskey; I don't want any more dope. I just want to tell her that before I die, because she has prayed for me for so many years and I've broken her heart so many times. I know it's too late for me, but won't you please help me tonight?"

God helped.

It wasn't easy. For weeks afterward I couldn't hold a glass of water but, like a dog, lapped it up out of a saucer. But God brought me through that night and through all the nights since that night in June of 1958.

After I had prayed, I just managed to stagger back to the bed and collapsed on it. I was lying there, almost in a dead faint, when the night nurse came in with some medicine.

"I don't want it," I said.

She was wide-eyed with amazement. "All you've been doing is yelling for this," she said. "You've been cursing the nurses and doctors, and now you don't want it. What's with you, anyhow?"

"I don't know, ma'am," I told her. "Tell me something. Are you a Christian?"

She nodded. "I think I am."

"If you are," I said, "would you pray for me?"

Now it was my turn to be amazed. Because she got right down there on her knees beside my bed and prayed.

Throughout that night, with the pangs of withdrawal eating my insides, and the hounds of hell chasing through my body, I didn't take any medication. I didn't know for sure what was happening to me. Yet even in my pitiful state I felt, somehow, a new fiber and a strange sensation of being purged. I even managed to fall asleep.

One of my first visitors in the bright light of a morning I had not expected to see was the chaplain, the Reverend Wylie Deal, a retired Baptist minister. He was carrying a Bible.

"There's something here I want you to read," he said.

I told him I couldn't read, but he propped me up and

then moved the Bible back and forth in front of my
eyes until I was able to make out the passage marked
by his finger. I can see it now with my eyes closed,
from Hebrews 13:5: ". . . for he hath said, I will never
leave thee, nor forsake thee."

It was, the chaplain said, something to hold on to. I
have held it to me ever since that morning, and I know
it to be God's truth.

Shortly afterward, the chaplain drew up a chair and
sat down beside me. "Johnny," he said, "would you go
to the chapel tonight and hear a good friend of yours?
He's coming out from town for a planned prayer meeting and I'd like you to hear him."

I couldn't imagine who it might be. "Who is this fellow, Chaplain?"

"He's a former golf pupil of yours, Emory Harper."

I knew him. Harper had won the state golf championship and had been "one of the boys." Then he had attended a Billy Graham revival and when he came back
to the club he wouldn't drink, smoke, or gamble any
more. We had all dropped him as a hopeless religious
fanatic. Personally I had treated him pretty badly,
taunting him in front of others and later cutting him
dead.

"Chaplain," I said, "that man doesn't want to see me."

"Yes, he does, and he's going to be here tonight."

"Well," I conceded, "I guess I'd go, but I don't think
they'll let me out of confinement."

"I'll take care of that," he promised, leaving. He returned a short while later pushing a wheel chair. Help-

ing me into it, he wheeled me out into a ward. "Now, you're out of confinement."

That evening I clambered laboriously from the wheel chair and made my way slowly toward the chapel. Again I would not let the aides or nurses help me. Just as I neared the chapel on my lonely journey of pain and weakness, the sky spun around me in a pinwheel of explosive colors and I fainted. Nobody noticed me and when I regained consciousness I pulled myself up against an oak tree. I had gashed my face in falling, and there was blood all over my robe and pajamas. But from the chapel I could hear the speaker reading from the Bible:

"For what shall it profit a man if he shall gain the whole world, and lose his own soul? Or what shall a man give in exchange for his soul?"

I knew I had to make another effort to reach the chapel. It took me a long time as I lurched from tree to tree toward the porch of the chapel; and as I stood there, clinging to a ladder leaning against the porch, a choir of young people was singing, "Just as I am, without one plea, but that thy blood was shed for me, O Lamb of God, I come."

Hauling myself up by the ladder, I managed to reach the doorway into the chapel. The door was open but I stood outside the screen door awhile. The choir had finished. Harper talked. Finally he said:

"Fellows, if there are any of you who are suffering today from fear or anxiety, or if you have anything wrong with you that you haven't been able to cure, turn it over to God. Let Jesus Christ take your burden, he who said, 'Come unto me all ye that labor and are heavy-laden, and I will give you rest.' Raise your hands as an indication that you want to receive him as your Saviour."

I knew that this was for me. I hadn't been able to open the door but, pressing up against the screen, I raised my hand. Harper, a little man but a powerful one, strode briskly down the aisle to the screen door where I was standing, opened it, and looked at me intently as the light from inside illuminated my haggard, emaciated condition.

"Aren't you Johnny Spence?"

"Yes, sir."

"Did you raise your hand?" he demanded.

"Yes, sir."

"Let me ask you something. Do you mean business? Understand, God means business, but do you?"

My voice shook. "Yes, sir. I meant it more than anything in the world when I raised my hand."

Harper threw his strong, muscular arms around me and pulled me inside. Then, holding me close, he said fervently, "Thank you, God. Thank you for Johnny Spence. I've been praying for him for more than eight years."

It was a statement that stunned me. This man I had disliked, and who I thought resented me, had been praying for me all this time.

We sat and talked for two hours in the chapel as he counseled me. I couldn't get over the wonder of his having prayed for me.

"I thought you'd hate me a lot for the things I've done to hurt you around here," I confessed. "I guess I've told everybody that you were some kind of a nut."

Harper smiled and gripped my hand. "No, Johnny. You see, when God came in and I accepted him, Christ transformed my mind, and all the bad things passed away. All things became new. When you know Jesus and he comes into your life, all things are transformed. Remember, Johnny, he is a loving Saviour and he is a living Saviour."

Later he took me back to my room, and when he had gone I felt suffused with a feeling of wonderful peace and contentment.

Understand this, now: just one night before, I had been standing on the threshold of death.

Four days later I was discharged from the hospital. I wasn't well and strong. My nerves twitched and trembled for weeks to come. But I had left the valley of the shadow behind me. Alcoholism and drug addiction were in the past because I had returned to God. Don't tell me about miracles.

It can be found in James 5:15, where it says: "and the Lord shall raise him up."

At the Spring Lake Club in Columbia,
S.C., 1965. Tim Hord, Charlotte, N.C.

2

Children, obey your parents in the Lord:
for this is right. *Ephesians 6:1*

The Job Came First

We were a happy, God-loving family, when I was a
boy in Columbia, South Carolina.

My father was superintendent of the Columbia Rail-
way Gas and Electric Company, in charge of streetcars. My mother was a devout woman and is now, at
eighty-one, the only living charter member of the
Lutheran Church of the Ascension.

There were three of us boys. I was the youngest;
Jim was six years older; and my other brother, Bob,
was three years older than I.

Through Mother's guidance we were constant in our church attendance. I remember her telling us, "Never put your church second. Never put God second. He is not a second-rate God. If you put him second, the Devil will surely come into your life."

I loved my father, and we all were inseparable. He took us hunting and fishing and always had an intense interest in whatever we boys were doing.

When I was almost six years old we moved from the center of town to Eau Claire, a suburb, and into a house only four blocks from the Ridgewood Country Club. That's where all of us started to caddy.

My brothers also sold newspapers, and it wasn't long before they were taking me along. Nobody understood how little Johnny sold more papers than his two bigger brothers combined. Even then I had a "gimmick." Somebody had taken me to the movies and I had seen Jackie Coogan in a picture called "The Kid" in which he was a ragged street urchin.

So I copied his gimmick. Little Johnny rolled down his stockings, put his cap on sideways, rubbed dirt all over his face—and kindly people took pity on me and bought my papers like hotcakes.

Until one day I asked a passerby to "help me out and buy a paper." The man gave me a searching look and asked me my name.

"Johnny Spence," I told him.

"Well, now," he said, "I only know one family of Spences in town. What's your daddy's name, son?"

"Jim Spence," I told him proudly.

"Is that the Jim Spence who's head of the streetcars?"
"Yes, sir," I nodded.

The man smiled, bought a paper, and walked away. What I didn't know was that he thought it was funny and called my father to tell him what I was doing. Within five minutes my father hove into view and he jerked a knot in my neck.

One night the Ridgewood Country Club burned down. The next day my brothers went over to look around, and they came home with the head of a spade mashie they had found. Jim took a limb from a hickory tree and fixed up a shaft for the club. My brothers took tomato cans and set them, open side up, into the ground of the baseball diamond behind our house. This provided a two-hole course, with a hole at each end of the diamond. That was the first look I ever had at anybody swinging a golf club.

One day I "borrowed" this prized club, and I was out there swinging away and having fun when they caught me. Then it wasn't much fun.

When I was about ten years old, I began to caddy at Ridgewood and later at the Columbia Country Club. Meanwhile we had extended our baseball-diamond golf course to three holes with pretty good sand greens. Jim, who was just sixteen at this time, obtained a job with the power company as a part-time dispatcher and bought himself a wooden-shafted set of "King Bee" clubs put out by a hardware company in Atlanta.

I thought they were the most beautiful things in the world, a number one wood, a midiron, mashie, spade mashie, and a putter. But he was so busy working that one day he gave them to me. I slept with the putter in bed beside me for weeks, and I was the happiest kid in the world.

Bob and I played whenever we could get a chance, and at fifteen he was winning all the tournaments for youngsters in the area. By the time he was seventeen he had been sponsored into the local club and was one of the best players in the state.

It was right around this time that Walter Hagen and Gene Sarazen came to Ridgewood to play an exhibition. Bob was chosen to play against them with Tommy Harmon, the winter professional at Camden, South Carolina.

I was in seventh heaven. Not only was Bob playing, but I had been given Sarazen's bag to carry, and I anticipated a big tip, maybe even as much as two dollars. I had to choke back the tears when Bob told the caddy master, "Send him home. He'll upset me."

So I lost the bag but I sneaked along behind the trees, loyally hoping that my big brother would win. He did, too. Bob scored an eagle on the fifteenth hole and then birdied the last three holes to win, one up. My financial loss forgotten, I was the proudest kid in town.

Then, when I was fourteen, a bomb burst in our happy family. I came home one afternoon to find my mother sitting on the porch. Tears streamed down her face and sobs racked her body. I was utterly astonished. "Mother, what's the matter?"

She dried her eyes, straightened up, and forced a

smile. But her voice broke again when she told me, "Your daddy has left home."

I was speechless and threw my arms around her. I had never thought there was anything wrong between my mother and father. When you're young and carefree, the hidden conflicts can go unnoticed, particularly if you have a blithe and happy-go-lucky nature such as I possessed; and such was my confidence, even then, that I hugged her close and reassured her.

"Don't you worry, Mother. I'll take care of you. I'll go right to the top and you'll never have to worry about anything." Boyishly I vowed to myself that I would make a million dollars and buy anything and everything for my mother that she might ever need. And, thinking of that moment, I know a deep shame at the probably even greater trials and tribulations I put her through later.

Although my father was gone, we managed handily. By the following year, when Bob was eighteen and I was fifteen, we played our way into the finals of the Columbia City golf championship against each other. Mother made us each a new pair of knickers for the playoff and then, knowing that we were always bickering with each other, gave us a stern lecture.

"Now I want you boys to be gentlemanly and don't fight with each other. If you don't fight, I'll give each of you two dollars."

Bob beat me, but we got through it without either of us charging at the other. Actually, having lost was a help to me. I worked harder than ever in my spare time to perfect my game, and within the next two years I forged quite a local reputation as a top-flight player. It seemed only natural to me in my vanity that, when I was only seventeen years old, through family contacts I was named to the vacant job as professional at the Ridgewood Country Club.

There was no doubt in my mind that I was on my way to fame and fortune.

When I became the professional at Ridgewood, I continued going to church and Sunday school every Sabbath, as well as to mid-week prayer meeting. It was a way of life I had always known and enjoyed.

Everything went along peacefully until, after about three months, I returned to the club one Sunday after taking mother home and found the club president waiting in the golf shop for me. Hands on hips, he stood blocking the doorway, and there was a deep frown on his face.

"Johnny," he growled, "where have you been? Boy, I've been looking all over for you."

I couldn't see where I had done anything wrong. "I've been to Sunday school and church."

"How long has this been going on?"

My manners had been pounded into me at an early age, yet even as a youngster I was always laughing and joking. So I grinned at him and answered lightly. "Mr. Joe, it's been going on just about as long as I can remember."

I smiled at him, but he didn't seem to think it was the least bit humorous and frowned even more darkly.

"Johnny, there's nothing wrong with church. I even belong to one myself. But your job must come first."

It is no excuse, but I was young, overwhelmed with my new importance, and really in ecstasy over my job.

"Yes sir, Mr. Joe. Thank you."

"Now next Sunday you be here all day," he admonished me. "And every Sunday after that. We like you, but we have the Governor of South Carolina, we have the Mayor of Columbia, we have all the industrial leaders and big merchants who work hard all week and come out here Sunday to relax. They expect you to be available. They pay you well and they like you. But if you can't be here, let me know and we'll get someone else for the job."

His tone was one of utter finality. I had only one recourse. "Yes sir, Mr. Joe. I'll be here."

I went inside, and my heart was heavy as I called my mother to tell her what had happened. Mother listened without interruption. Then she spoke to me calmly and quietly.

"Son, I've been expecting this ever since you took that job. Golf is a great game, a wonderful game, and I know how much you love it. But God is wonderful, too, and he must come first. The Bible says in John 3:30 that 'He must increase, but I must decrease,' so you have to constantly think of God as being first in your life."

I was young and stubborn. "Mother, I'll find a way. I'm a strong boy and I can make this thing by myself."

"No, you can't," she said sadly. "You can't make it by yourself, son. You know, God says in Matthew 6:33, 'But seek ye first the kingdom of God, and his righteousness; and all these things shall be added unto you.'

Son, everything you want, God will give to you if you look to him."

I just couldn't let myself give up this job that meant so much to me. "Mother, I have a car. We're paying for a house. We're being fed by this job."

Mother's voice was firm. "Son, we had a house and these other things before you got this job. You just give up that job and come home right now."

I couldn't see it. "Mother, I just can't."

"Let me amplify a couple more verses for you," she pleaded. "These are God's words. Listen to God, not your mother."

Right there, on the phone, she read to me from Mark 8:36: "For what shall it profit a man, if he shall gain the whole world, and lose his own soul?"

There was a moment's silence, and Mother asked me, "Johnny, what will it profit you if you get all these things and lose your own self? And, Johnny, what will you receive in exchange for your soul?"

I couldn't argue with this kind of reasoning. I simply hung up the phone and went back to work in the golf shop.

I had always been very close to Mother. I never left her, or hung up, without telling her I loved her. This time I hadn't. In thinking only of this job, I had forgotten all about love.

That day I hung up the phone on Almighty God. I had stepped out from behind the shield of faith, ignoring the advice in Ephesians 6:16: "Above all, taking the shield of faith, wherewith ye shall be able to quench all the fiery darts of the wicked."

Mother had read this to me many times, telling me that when this shield of faith is thin, it becomes thin because you walk away from God. And it started for me the day I listened to the president of that club, thinking of money and glamour, instead of listening to my mother, who was reading from God's word.

After I'd hung up the phone on my mother and turned away from God that afternoon, we went out to play an exhibition. Every Sunday afternoon in either Columbia or Camden, a nearby town, we would play exhibition matches. Normally, these matches started off with just a few dollars at stake. But gradually we raised the stakes until we were playing each Sunday for thousands of dollars.

We would have a $1,000 Nassau, meaning $1,000 on each nine holes and an extra $1,000 for the total match. Then there would be "presses" on the final few holes by those who were trailing, as well as a great many other kinds of side bets. Usually my brother Bob and I would play two other professionals, although often I would take one of my members and play another professional and one of his members.

Very seldom did my team lose these matches. I was a pretty sharp gambler. Everybody likes to win, but I seemed to have the faculty of playing best under pressure. I didn't see anything wrong in taking advantage of any available "sucker," either. If I knew I could shoot par and my opponent was close to it, I'd play him even. If I thought I could beat him by seven shots, well, I'd give him one, maybe. So I was gambling heavily, but primarily on sure things. And I didn't see anything wrong with clipping anybody who would hold still for it.

Obviously, it hadn't taken me long to forsake the way of the Lord or the teachings of my mother. Of course I knew it then, but I recall it now with a heavy heart, that she had always admonished us how, in Proverbs 6:17, we are told to beware of "a proud look, a lying tongue."

I went brashly ahead. Yes, I made a lot of money. But I spent it unwisely, too.

Not long afterward, I was offered a job teaching golf at the University of South Carolina in conjunction with my duties as golf professional at Ridgewood Country Club, later to become known as the Columbia Country Club.

The dean of women came to the club one afternoon and asked me if I would teach 47 girls at the university, holding classes on the campus. It was to be instituted as a regular course; I would not only teach them how to play golf, but also grade them on their application and improvement.

Having a natural eye for the ladies and feeling that I was a pretty big-time operator, I accepted this extra job without qualms, even though most of my "pupils" would be somewhat older than I was. Of course it wasn't long before I became attracted to one of them in particular. It started when she came to me one afternoon and asked whether she could skip class to go uptown.

I won't mention her name, because she was a local girl and from one of what are called the "best" families.

The top of her blond head came just above my shoulders, and deep blue eyes looked at me provocatively from a heart-shaped face. On this particular day she leaned her lithesome body against me mockingly.

"I've torn my hose, professor," she said archly, lifting her skirt high and extending a shapely leg. "Won't you please let me go so I can buy some new stockings?"

Of course, all this attention had long since turned my head, and I was filled with egotism and an enlarged sense of my own importance.

"Let me go, Johnny," she smiled, "and I'll bake you a cake."

Which she did, a few days later, and invited me over to her sorority house. It wasn't long until we were dating steadily, going to the college dances on Saturday nights at the Block C Club, the athletic club at the university which held dances in the old gymnasium.

We went to these dances for many weeks, and then one night she told me she wasn't going to have any more dates with me.

"I'm sorry, Johnny," she said, "but everybody thinks you're a sissy."

"A what?" I asked, dumfounded.

"A sissy," she repeated. "Everybody says you're pretty dull and sissified because you won't even take a drink or smoke a cigarette. Why, you don't even laugh at funny stories."

During the dances, it was the practice at the intermissions to go out to where the cars were parked. A dozen boys and girls would mix drinks, or drink right out of bottles. Of course I was in their company, but I had never taken a drink. Usually I just stood around, trying to join in the talk, but always I was glad when the intermission was over.

Now, as we stood on the side of the dance floor and she accused me of being a sissy, I was hurt at first and then became extremely angry. The crowd was filing back onto the floor and the music started up, but I just stood there like a post.

"Well," she said again, "they've been talking about me for a long time. They say I'm the only co-ed here who is dating a sissy."

That was too much and I started to take off my coat. "All right, I'll show them who's a sissy," I told her. "There's the varsity fullback right over there. Hold this coat and I'll punch him right on the nose, right here and now. Maybe he'll kill me, but they'll know I'm no coward and no sissy."

She grabbed my coat by the lapels and pulled it back on my shoulders. "Don't be a jackass," she said, looking around in embarrassment. "That won't prove anything except that you're common."

"Well, how can they call me a sissy if I take a swing at the biggest man in the place?" I argued.

"I don't mean that way, silly. It's just that everybody says it, and I know it's true, that you won't even drink a glass of wine. That you won't even have a bottle of beer, a sociable highball, or even a cocktail at the parties and at the fraternity houses. You won't even smoke a ciga- rette, and it's noticeable that when somebody tells an off-color joke you won't even laugh but even turn away sometimes. So I'm being looked down on. Johnny, I like you and we have fun together, but I can't go with somebody who is peculiar like that. So this is our last night."

I was at a loss for words; then they spurted out. "What do you want me to do? I'm trying to be an athlete, a good golf professional. Why, in high school, the coach came in and told us that it was all right for him to smoke but that if he caught any of the boys doing it he'd fire them off the team even if there was nobody left to play. I have a long way to go, and I want to be a big success, and I have every desire to live right. That's why I don't do these things. But can't you like me for what I am? I'm real gone on you, so I wish you would. Honestly, honey, I really love you. Won't you go with me without drinking?"

What I said, I could see, had made little impression on her.

"I'm sorry, Johnny. If you'd just be sociable and do a little of it, I could do a lot of things for you. You'd be surprised at what I'd do for you if you'd just do this little thing for me. I want to be with you but I can't this way."

We stood there on the side of the dance floor, couples swirling past us, and I stared hard at her. Meanwhile, other thoughts began to go through my mind. What did she mean, she could "do a lot of things" for me? Our relationship had been completely platonic, except for a bit of very amateurish petting. Yet, nearing eighteen, I was feeling stirrings inside me, and she was completely desirable to me.

Then, too, her father was on the board of directors at

the Riverside Country Club and, in essence, one of my bosses. There was no doubt that he could cause me to lose my job. I had to look at the two pictures—my mother's earlier training, and my decision to make my own way and take my own chances in favor of money and position.

I didn't feel as if I had been away from church very long, although I hadn't been there in months. I'd been away from the Christian influence and atmosphere created by my mother. I hadn't been around a minister or heard a Christian song. Mother once told me if I left the armor of God, the shield of faith that I had in God, pretty soon the fiery darts of the wicked one would come through and hit me.

The Book of Ephesians 6:16 tells us about this in God's words: "Above all, taking the shield of faith, wherewith ye shall be able to quench all the fiery darts of the wicked."

But that night I saw my car, my job, my girl friend, everything that I wanted, going out the window because I wasn't doing what this girl wanted me to do.

Looking back now, I think of that night with great regret, wishing now that I had remembered Romans 12:1–2:

"I beseech you therefore, brethren, by the mercies of God, that ye present your bodies a living sacrifice, holy, acceptable unto God, which is your reasonable service.

"And be not conformed to this world: but be ye transformed by the renewing of your mind, that ye may prove what is that good, and acceptable, and perfect, will of God."

I knew it then. But I chose to ignore it.

"All right," I told her. "I'll do it your way."

She reached up and kissed me on the cheek, and then cuddled close to me as we moved slowly out into the throng on the dance floor.

When intermission came we went outside as usual. Only this time I held out my hand for a cup of whiskey and water. She held my arm tight against her, looking at me proudly, as I raised it to my lips.

Thus did I take my first drink of alcohol. Not much urging was required, either, to make me smoke my first cigarette.

The whiskey didn't make me sick. I didn't die. As a matter of fact, I thought the slightly giddy sensation which soon came over me was rather pleasant. I was buoyed up by the feeling that I was a big man; one of the "crowd"; finally accepted fully by my friends. Later on that night, in my new-found exhilaration, I pushed one of the boys into a swimming pool with all his clothes on and was pushed in myself. We were hilarious.

That night on which I took my stand to go with those who walk down the broad, wide road of conformity sums up the beginning of how I started drinking—and worse. As a starter, as she had promised, she "did a lot of things" for me. Everything.

If I had but read Proverbs 14:12 with my heart and true understanding, my life would have been altered greatly. For it says: "There is a way which seemeth right unto a man, but the end thereof are the ways of death."

There is a great sadness within me as I look back at
that night on which I fell. For this lovely girl also went
on to become an alcoholic and in her bleak despair,
long after we had drifted apart, took her own life. It is
a sordid story which Proverbs 7:27 sums up in a few
words:

"Her house is the way to hell, going down to the
chambers of death."

Spence (right) at fifteen and brother, Bob, at eighteen, posing at the Columbia City Championship meet in knickers made by their mother for the occasion.

3

Wine is a mocker, strong drink is raging:
and whoever is deceived thereby is not wise.
Proverbs 20:1

You're in the Army Now

I stayed on at Ridgewood as the professional for a little more than a year, and it was a riotous time. Now that I had learned about women, all of them seemed fair game. Now that I had learned about liquor, I was taking a postgraduate course in drinking. My girl friend objected to the first and thought I was too good a student in the second, provoking an argument that finally split us.

Feeling sorry for myself, and having a pocketful of money, I quit my job on the theory that it was time I saw a little more of the world. Briefly I took on the challenging job of finishing a course at Hartsville, South Carolina. I stayed on awhile giving lessons, teaching as many as a dozen or more people a day. Finally I got tired of that, went on a spree, and ended up in Miami. From there I caught a boat to New York and finally wound up back in South Carolina at the Florence Country Club. Soon I was off again on another bender and another trip.

On my twentieth birthday I awoke in a Bowery hotel in New York City and, taking stock of myself, decided that the best thing I could do, the thing I wanted most, was to see my mother. So I went back to Columbia, where she was working in a cafeteria. It was so nice to be back with her that I took a job as a doorman in a theater. However, I kept on drinking and it was no secret in a city of that size.

My father by this time had become chief of the claims department for the South Carolina Electric and Gas Company. One night, as I headed home after a drinking session, I ran into him on the street.

"Hello, Johnny," he greeted me. Then, seeing my condition, he asked, "Son, is there anything I can do for you?"

I cursed him and turned my back and started to walk away.

"Remember," he called after me, "if you want it, I have a job for you."

When I sobered up, I went to see him and he arranged for me to become a night bus dispatcher. Soon I began driving a bus myself.

One afternoon I was having lunch in the cafeteria where my mother worked, when I looked up and saw the prettiest girl I'd ever seen in my life. Pretty? She was gorgeous: tall, statuesque, creamy skin, and a wonderful smile.

"Ma," I asked, "who is that girl?"

My mother smiled at me and told me her name was Dorothy Foster. She was from Charleston, West Virginia, and while working as a laboratory technician for a local doctor was living with her brother, Ernest Foster. He was director of manual arts in the Columbia city schools. As Southern archery champion he had been the inventor of archery golf.

For five days in a row I asked her for a date. For five days in a row she refused. I was so persistent that finally she told me, "Your own aunt told me you were a no-good roughneck and to stay away from you."

"Ah, now, honey,"—I gave her my number one personality smile—"she's one of those religious nuts who don't want anybody to have fun."

Dottie was furious. "She's a fine woman, and let me tell you, Mr. Spence, there are more ways to have what you call fun without drinking and heaven knows what."

"What do you mean, 'heaven knows what'?" I asked her teasingly.

She blushed and walked away from me.

Then one day, a short while later, she got on my bus. It was practically empty and when she paid her fare I asked her for a date. She ignored me and went back to a seat. When it came time for her to get off, I didn't open the door. Instead I asked her, "When?"

She didn't answer, so I drove to the next stop. Some-one got off through the rear door and Dottie tried to rush back that way, but I closed the door again.

"When?" I asked her.

She didn't answer, so I drove on to the next stop. By this time it was even getting to be funny to her. Sud-denly she broke into laughter and came up and took a seat near me.

"All right. You win. Tonight will be fine."

During my boyhood days, when my father was su-perintendent of streetcars for the power company, he often took me to the car barns with him. I was a privi-leged character, naturally, and the master mechanic let me ride on the switching car and finally even taught me how to drive a streetcar. I knew most of the motor-men and one of the first things I did, being a showoff, was to take Dottie for a ride on one of the few remain-ing streetcars. The motorman, a long-time friend, sat in the back smoking a cigar and let me drive.

It took three years of courting before Dottie agreed to become engaged to me. I didn't drink in front of her, or when I had a date with her, because she was set against it. But shortly after we were engaged I went to pick her up one night slightly drunk. She gave me an icy look and handed back my ring.

"This is it," she said. "Everybody told me you were a roughneck but I wouldn't listen."

"Please," I begged. "Keep the ring and I won't drink any more. I promise." She kept the ring, and for a while I didn't touch a drink.

We were married, and with both of us working we

were saving money. I had an itch to get back into golf. Dottie went right along with me because I told her how wonderful it would be. Eventually we acquired 185 acres on a hill overlooking the city and built the Riverside Country Club. To get some ideas on construction, as well as to arrange some other details, I went to Florida. While there, through some friends, I met Bernarr MacFadden, the widely known physical culturist, in Miami Beach. It was a meeting that was to have a tragic effect on me at a future date, but more of that later.

We opened our Riverside Country Club in September of 1941, and on Pearl Harbor Day three months later had a total of 338 members. One year later we had ten members left, most of them having enlisted or been drafted.

Columbia meanwhile had become a giant air base for B-25's and there was a huge camp at Fort Jackson. Bars were illegal in the state, but I bypassed this by getting a federal license to convert our club into an officers' club. This gave me carte blanche and I went all out. I had a swinging bar, and slot machines all over the place. I also had the foresight to load up my cellar with whiskey, and I figured I was solidly in business. I was, too, because I had many cases of half-pints of liquor that cost me $39.95 per case. Within six weeks it was bringing $90 a case and skyrocketed up from there.

With the officers it was one big gay party on the old gladiatorial theory of eat, drink, and be merry, because tomorrow you die. Johnny joined right in with them and helped them get rid of their money. As long as they bought it, I drank it. It came right close to getting me killed at one point in the summer of 1942.

A captain friend of mine flew over from the air base in a light two-seater training plane, and landed on a fairway near the clubhouse. We had a few drinks and were feeling no pain when he suggested we take a little spin. In short order we climbed into the plane and he started to take off. But then he saw we weren't going to make it before we hit a plowed field, so he cut the motor. There was a tremendous thump and we nosed clean over in the plowed field. Neither of us was hurt, but the plane was a wreck and they had to send over a truck and crew to get it out. The captain was transferred overseas very shortly thereafter.

Looking back, I know I was lucky that I wasn't killed. Because now there is no question in my mind but that I would have gone straight to hell. As it says in Revelations 22:20, "Surely I come quickly." Well, I surely would have gone the other way quickly.

However, my little gold mine finally ran second to Uncle Sam when I was drafted into the Army in 1943. I didn't want to close down the club because it was doing so well. When word got around that I had to leave, a man I'll call Bill O'Donald came to see me. He told me his father had been a Baptist minister, and suggested that I hire him to run the club on a share basis. It sounded pretty good to me, so I agreed. I stored away for future use 140 dozen prewar golf balls and sixteen complete sets of golf clubs, items that were to come in mighty handy from time to time later when equipment was impossible to get.

With everything neatly tied up, I thought, I hauled out for Fort Bragg in Fayetteville, North Carolina, where I was instructed to report for induction. I took with me a case of quarts of whiskey. Well, the first thing that happened when I arrived was that I encountered a group of officers who had been "members" at my club, and when I broke out the whiskey they took me to the officers' club for a party which delayed my induction two days.

The party had hardly ended when I was summoned by a WAAC lieutenant who had been a singer with Fred Waring's band.

"There's a golf tournament at Pinehurst and you are to represent Fort Bragg," she instructed me.

"Yes, ma'am," I said, trying to look real military in my civvies.

I had a private fitting for a uniform and, on top of that, not even having been inducted, and sans dog tag and shots, I received a five-day furlough for the tournament. It snowballed even more than that because when the officers learned that I could get golf balls and liquor, I received any and all favors I requested. I really like this man's Army pretty well, I decided.

Without too much trouble I wound up in the base athletic program along with such fellows as Ernie White of the St. Louis Cardinals, Buster Maynard of the Giants, Van Lingle Mungo of the Brooklyn Dodgers, Jake Early of the Washington Senators, and Norm Brown of the Philadelphia Athletics. We took basic training together, and when the division was shipped out we stayed right there.

We almost ruined it one night when Ernie, Van and I got high and felt belligerent.

"We'll go see the officer of the day, or the night, or whatever he is," Ernie suggested with liquid determination. We were right with him, a trio of plastered patriots.

Stumbling along, we finally found the O.D.'s quarters and knocked on the door in a thunderous demand for attention. He was obviously surprised when he came to the door and saw us.

"Just where is the fighting the thickest?" Ernie demanded.

"Why," said the startled O.D., "I guess in North Africa."

"That's fine," Ernie asserted. "We want to be sent there immediately."

The O.D. happened to be a friend of ours. "We'll talk it over in the morning," he said. Fortunately that was the end of it.

Meanwhile, I had been assigned to give golf instruction to the officers, and Dottie came up to run the golf shop for me. We had a room right over the golf shop, which adjoined the officers' club annex, where the officers and visiting VIPs ate. I couldn't get in there, of course, but Dottie could.

At one period there was a great deal of excitement around the post because of two distinguished guests. One was General George C. Marshall, and with him was Winston Churchill. Dottie ate right in there where they were. I had my dinner sitting on the back steps.

Our special unit at last ran into trouble when we

put on a baseball game against the 100th Division. We had 22 men. The division had 15,000 men. At the start of the fourth inning we were beating them 14 to 0. The commanding general couldn't take it any more. He stormed down out of the stands and stopped the game. The word leaked out that night that he had called Washington and demanded that our "band of professionals" be disbanded. That was the end of our special unit, as we were all called in and shipped to different stations. I hastily pulled a few strings and got myself sent back to Fort Jackson.

I simply had to get back home, because word had been reaching me that O'Donald, who was running my club on a percentage basis, had turned it into a real clip joint. Customers were being given knockout drops, beaten up and rolled, and a number of people had been badly hurt. At this time I was a corporal and, of course, my club was open to officers only. We weren't supposed to be out of uniform, but I changed into golf clothes anyhow as soon as I got back to Columbia. Then I drove over to see O'Donald.

It goes without saying that he wasn't happy to see me. Particularly when I let him have it without any preliminary small talk.

"I hear some mighty bad things about how you're running this place," I said. "Well, I'm back, and I'll tell you right now that you're going to clean things up."

He was an arrogant, mean-eyed man, but smooth or rough as the occasion demanded. "Have a drink," he said.

"Fine," I told him.

Knowing the reputation of the place, I took one cautious sip and knew he was being fancy with me. It was loaded with knockout drops.

"I should bury this glass in your skull," I said. "But all I'm gonna do is run you right out of here."

O'Donald's bouncers had sidled over in our direction and were standing nearby, obviously ready to give me a working over. Lighting a cigar and blowing smoke in my face, he let me know exactly where I stood.

"Buster, you're the one who's going to be run out of here. You don't have a chance. I've got the MPs and the police in my hip pocket. And, on top of that, they're gonna ship you overseas. I've already taken care of that."

I had to fight my temper to keep from laying him out with a chair and taking on everybody else who wanted some. But I knew I couldn't win against these odds, so I got up and left without a word.

The first thing I did was to go see the sheriff, an old friend of mine, but he simply shrugged his shoulders. "I can't move him. He has a federal license."

There was another fellow in town, known as a pretty rugged customer, who had been in the same business. So I went to see him and asked him if he'd like to take over the club and run it for me.

"How you gonna get O'Donald out?" he asked. "You know how long it will take with lawyers and all that."

Obviously he, too, was afraid of O'Donald and his hoodlums. But by this time I'd had all I could stand.

First of all I got myself half high early the next afternoon. The fairways had grown up in silage and I meant to cut it, knowing full well that O'Donald would challenge me. But I was determined that I'd blow him and all his hoodlums off my property if I had to do it. Somewhere I'd picked up a sniper's rifle that I could pick your teeth with at 500 yards. Then I also loaded my double-barreled 20-gauge shotgun and stuck a .38-caliber police pistol in my jacket pocket. Then I drove to the club and parked right near the entrance.

Getting out the tractor, I climbed aboard and, holding my rifle and shotgun across my lap, drove along the driveway. I had it timed perfectly because there came O'Donald and his two bouncers riding up in a big black Cadillac.

"What you figurin' to do?" he demanded as he pulled up and stopped near the tractor.

"I'm gonna cut on 18."

"You can't do that without my permission," he growled, starting to open the door and get out of his car.

With one hand I aimed the shotgun squarely at him while I covered the two bouncers with the sniper's rifle.

"You open that door and I'm gonna unload," I promised. "I'm done foolin' with you and your monkeys, O'Donald, and if you don't believe it, just climb out of that hearse and I'll put all three of you in another one."

I wasn't kidding and they knew it. All three of them froze, and O'Donald's voice was placative when he suggested, "Let's talk this over, Johnny."

"We're done talkin'," I growled. "And I'll tell you something else. I'm comin' over here tonight and take back the club. You'd better believe that, too. Now turn that hearse around and get out of here."

My shotgun must have looked like the twin tubes of the Holland Tunnel to him, and they couldn't have been getting any comfort out of the snake's eye of that sniper's rifle, either. Because O'Donald started cursing a blue streak, slammed the car door he had started to open, and wheeled the car around and drove off.

Early that evening I stuffed my .38 into my jacket pocket and got together two carloads of my friends for my "party" at the club. We juiced it up a little and were in rare form by the time we roared up to the club and piled out of the cars. At the head of my little army I barged into the club, which was going full tilt, and walked right up to O'Donald. He was a tough fellow, but he knew the game was over.

"Out!" I shouted. "I'm gonna give you just about ten seconds to be on your way."

His two bouncers had started to move toward the noise; but when they saw us they decided discretion was much the better part of valor and, like all their breed, headed for the kitchen and the back door. White-faced, O'Donald followed them with me on his heels. As we entered the kitchen, the bouncers had already fled into the night. At this point, O'Donald whipped out a pistol and shot out a large light over one of the stoves.

There was a string of small light bulbs around the ceiling. I pulled out my .38 and, slamming him up against the wall said, "That kind of target is for little boys, not a big fellow like me. It takes a man to get those little ones."

Then I proceeded to shoot out three of the small bulbs. As the glass tinkled down, I whipped around and held the pistol on him. For a few seconds it was a question as to whether we were going to gun each other.

"Out!" I growled, nodding toward the open back door.

O'Donald angrily stuffed his gun in his pocket and walked out. I followed, watching until he got into his car and raced away.

It was typical of the roughhouse antics that had been going on at the club that the shots hadn't even attracted anyone into the kitchen. I walked back inside and joined my friends in a celebration they'd already started at the bar.

Looking back on that incident, I am ashamed at how close I came to killing a fellow man. Possibly it may be true that with that type of person you cannot turn the other cheek. Yet I am certain that had I turned to the due processes of law I would have had no difficulty retrieving my property.

It says in Psalms 18:48: "He delivereth me from mine enemies: yea, thou liftest me up above those that rise up against me: thou hast delivered me from the violent man."

But I was the violent man. It was to be a long time before I was ready to accept the fact and he delivered me.

For about six months I ran the club and, with the end of the war, was discharged from the Army in November of 1945. Of course, with the end of the war, my "officers' club" started to draw fire from local and state authorities. In the gubernatorial race I backed the wrong man, and retribution was swift. I lost my license.

Meanwhile, Steve Duda, an accomplished golf professional, had come to work with me and we opened a nine-hole course. But with no more liquor or gambling and too little play, it was too costly. I probably would have tried a little bootlegging and a private "game," but there always were two constables on hand to watch this spot, which had been a wartime cesspool. So eventually I decided to sell the club.

When I did, it was, of course, an occasion for another drinking party as a sort of celebration. It was a two-day bender at the end of which Kirby Higbe and I wound up in a spot in Camden, South Carolina, where they had an orchestra. Kirby was worried about whether he would be able to pitch again, and I began needling him that he didn't have a chance. Finally it really got under his skin.

The band was pumping away when all of a sudden he downed the whiskey in a shot glass, stood up, picked up the glass, cranked up in his windup, and fired the shot glass right through the bass drum.

"What do you mean I can't pitch?" he yelled. "That was a perfect strike with the best fast ball you'll ever see."

They made an even better pitch. They threw both of us out bodily.

Looking back on all of this, there is great meaning for me in Proverbs 23:35.

"They have stricken me, shalt thou say, and I was not sick; they have beaten me, and I felt it not: when shall I awake?"

With wife, Dottie, who is getting a golf lesson during their stay at Dansville, N.Y., Golf Club, 1947, as guests of Bernarr Macfadden.

4

Look not thou upon the wine . . .
Proverbs 23:31

A Mental Case

Early in 1946 I decided to try my hand on the professional golf tour, certain that I could play well enough to hold my own against the best of them. But I was in for quite a shock. At this time I was on a brandy kick, and as the tour moved from the winter tournaments on the West Coast into the South for the spring events, my brandy nerves simply wouldn't let me play anywhere near as well as I knew I should.

Somewhere or other I heard about a physical culture hotel at Danville, New York, which was operated by

Bernarr MacFadden, the man I had met in Miami Beach a number of years earlier. I discussed it with Dottie and we decided that it might straighten me out if I went there, because what I needed was not medicine but to regain my health and steady my nerves. Dottie remained at home and I went to Danville.

For a month and a half I was off liquor and worked myself into marvelous condition. There was a ten-mile hike before breakfast, good food, salt baths, and plenty of exercise and rest. At the end of six weeks I was a new man and happily telephoned Dottie to meet me in New York two days later, which was a Monday.

Sunday morning, as I was preparing to leave the hotel, one of the guests I had been friendly with suggested that we go to church.

"They're having communion in the Lutheran Church and I don't want to go alone," he said.

"Fine," I agreed, and innocently we went off to church on that lovely Sunday morning.

As a boy of five I had been baptized by Dr. W. H. Greever, the founder of our Lutheran Church. During services I had pumped the organ, and many times I had helped the minister fill the communion cups with grape juice. I had never given it much consideration, but I figured that all churches used grape juice for communion services.

But the church I went to on this bright Sunday— feeling clean and whole and healthy once again—used wine in its communion services. I didn't realize it at the time, but that little cup of wine I drank triggered my lurking thirst. Dr. Martin Kissen of the Saul Clinic for Alcoholism in Philadelphia told me later that even a drop of shaving lotion trickling into the mouth of an alcoholic is enough to start him drinking again.

That communion wine did the same to me. For as I drove down to New York, where I was to meet Dottie the next day, I kept craving a drink. When I arrived in New York I met Johnny (Scat) Davis, a bandleader friend of mine, and still didn't have a drink as I fought off the urge through the help of our conversation. Finally I went to bed, still without a drink.

Dottie arrived early the next morning, and I had arranged for us to have breakfast with some friends of ours. But as we left the hotel, Dottie slipped off the curb and tore her stocking.

An ordinary accident, and I should have been concerned about her. Instead it enraged me. I know why now. It gave me an excuse to have that drink I'd been wanting so badly. Thus when we arrived at the restaurant for breakfast with our waiting friends, I didn't eat.

"Bring me a glass of wine," I ordered the waiter. "A big one. No, on second thought, bring a bottle."

The label on the bottle which he brought said "Christian Brothers." To a mind like mine that seemed to make it all right. So I really started to guzzle it. Soon I ordered a second bottle. After that I don't remember too much except that I told Dottie I had some things to do around New York and that she should go back to Columbia. Anxiously she tried to get me to go with her, pleading and begging me to stop drinking, but her tears only sent me off in another fit of violent anger and I walked out.

Ten days later I got as far as Baltimore, where I continued drinking with friends, and then went on to Washington for more of the same. Finally I got to Fayetteville and, after three days of drinking alone in a hotel, for the first time had the delirium tremens.

I screamed and rolled on the floor and tore up the furniture. When the manager protested, I barred the door and told him to go away or I'd kill somebody. The management called Dottie and she drove up to get me. Only when I heard her voice at the door did I finally let them come in.

This woman I love so much was a saint. There were no recriminations and no tears. She led me out like a little boy, got me into the car, and drove me home. Putting me to bed, she called our family doctor as well as my mother.

Mothers are always mothers and mine was angry with me. "Is this the reason you went to that physical culture hotel?" she demanded tartly. "What kind of a place is that?"

The doctor recommended that I be put in a private hospital in Aiken. I was in such a state of shock, and so weak, that I didn't know what was going on when they took me to this private sanitarium. It was an old estate surrounded by high walls; the huge iron gates were locked and guarded by a watchman.

Only after I was inside the front door and had been helped up to the second floor did I start to notice my surroundings. Then, all of a sudden, I was terrified.

There were bars on the windows and I felt as if I were in prison.

Just as I thought I was going to jump out of my skin, the doctor came in. With some surprise I recognized him as a psychiatrist who had been an Army doctor at Fort Bragg when I was there. Even at that time I hadn't particularly liked him.

"You're going to be all right," he said. "You're a bit disturbed and we're going to treat you."

"Bunk," I told him. "I've just been drunk. That's all."

He tried to soothe me. "Don't worry, we're going to help you. Just take it easy."

With that he left me alone in the room and I began to pace up and down. What I needed, I thought, was a drink. So I went out in the corridor in search of the doctor. He must be downstairs, I figured, but as I reached the head of the stairway and started down, a hulking attendant in a white uniform appeared from around a corner and grabbed me by the arm.

"Back in your room," he ordered roughly.

"Take your paws off me," I told him angrily. "I want to see the doctor."

"You'll have to wait."

"I don't mean to wait at all," I shouted. "You get the doctor or it's going to be one of us standing here. I mean I'm going down and see him right now."

I'd been shouting so loudly that the doctor appeared at the foot of the stairs.

"Captain," I yelled, "I got to see you right now."

He came up the stairs and I told him, "I've got to see my wife right now."

His reply stopped me cold for a moment. "You can't. You've been committed."

I stuttered. "Committed? Who committed me?"

"Your family."

Now I got madder than before. "They're the ones who ought to be committed. Why, I'll . . ."

"Just a second now," the doctor interrupted, "and we're going to give you some medicine."

Then, for the first time, I was introduced to drugs.

The doctor gave me a big jolt of paraldehyde, and before I had taken three breaths I was out stone-cold unconscious.

When I awoke, I was strapped to my bed. It was morning and they moved me downstairs and gave me a shock treatment. After it was over, they moved me back upstairs and I was so weak and exhausted that I thought to myself, boy, you must really be nuts. My mind was cluttered with confusion and I couldn't seem to think. I was on the verge of giving up completely.

But then, as I calmed down in the next couple of days and finally was permitted out of bed, I saw one poor fellow who was insane. It shook me to the core and I began to wonder all over again if I was insane. It gave me the shakes. Then, in succession, I ranted to myself in anger at Dottie and my mother. Frustration at my helpless position only added to the flames.

Then I found a friend.

He was a fellow from Columbia who was a drunk

just like me. He, too, had been committed for "drying out" and, like me, had seriously begun to wonder whether he was demented.

"I'm not crazy, are you?" I whispered.

He shook his head. "I don't think so. But sometimes I get to wondering when I look around this creepy joint."

We were kindred spirits.

"We've got to get out of here," I told him.

"Yeah," he agreed, "but how?"

It took us a few days to work it out, but then the perfect opportunity presented itself when we were ordered out into the yard to rake leaves in what was described to us as "physical therapy."

"How do you feel?" I asked him, wondering if this were the right time to make our escape attempt.

"Great," he told me. "I'm ready for whatever you say."

"We'll blitz the guy at the gate," I said. "I stole a bottle of paraldehyde and I've got it in my pocket. You talk to him and I'll cold-cock him from behind."

"But we haven't any money and we'll really look nuts running up the street in these pajamas and bathrobes," he protested.

"It'll be okay. Don't worry," I told him hopefully.

My co-conspirator and I industriously raked our way right up to the gate where the guard was standing. Then he stopped and began making conversation with the guard. Silently I moved up behind him and, hitting him on the head with the bottle, knocked him cold. Within seconds we snatched the gate key, unlocked the

gate and swung it open, and began running up the
street with our robes flapping out behind us.

We hadn't gone far, huffing and puffing and looking
back over our shoulders, when a lady drove up beside
us and called out, "What's the matter?"

"They're trying to kill us back in that nuthouse," I
shouted.

"Get in," she said, stopping the car. "I've heard some
bad stories about that place. I'll take you to a friend's
house and you can telephone your families."

She drove us to a house on the outskirts of town and
both of us called home. Dottie answered the telephone.

"Listen," I told her quite calmly, "I'm not mad. But
if somebody doesn't come down here and get me and
apologize, then I'm really going to get mad. I'll apologize for everything I did and I'll try real hard to do
better. But I want you to know it's not as bad as what
you all have been doing to me."

My friend's family came for him, and Dottie came
and got me.

This first trip to an institution of this sort made me
realize for the first time that I was regarded as a mental
case in the eyes of the public. It is a confusion experienced by millions who do not realize that they are
alcoholics and are told instead that they are "disturbed"
or are made to feel that they are demented.

I went "crazy" only when I was drinking. If this was
due to alcohol, I tried to reason with myself, why
couldn't I use my brain and abstain from alcohol? The
answer, as I see it, was that there was nothing to which
I could cling.

In what I have to say here, I am not attacking Alcoholics Anonymous. It is a step in the right direction, but the major fault is that A.A. never gets into the spiritual phase of saving an alcoholic.

A.A.'s record is perfect. Yet that is due to the fact that you are a member only when you are sober. They'll come at midnight and talk to you. They are good and they try. But they help only while they are there with you, holding your hand.

When I get shaky, holding the Bible in my hand is all that I really need. I have found, at long last, that Christ is the Saviour and all the help I need is in the Bible. He tells us that "I shall never forsake nor leave thee."

Read it for yourself in Isaiah 26:4: "Trust ye in the Lord for ever: for in the Lord Jehovah is everlasting strength."

Once, after I had finally been saved, Billy Graham put his arm around me and asked, "How long were you in A.A.?"

"Nine years."

"What happened?"

"I stayed drunk nine years."

"Didn't you say to me that Jesus Christ was the answer to alcoholism?"

"Yes," I replied. "I did."

That conversation cost me a job almost immediately. Dr. Graham used it in his column, which appeared in a Charleston newspaper. That same day it appeared in print I went to see some people who were going to build a golf course near Charleston and had asked me to appear for an interview in connection with doing the job.

I knew something was wrong shortly after we got together. Finally one of the group blurted out, "Do you drink liquor?"

"No," I told them.

"Aren't you a booze hound?" another insisted.

"No, I am not," I said.

"You know a fellow named Billy Graham?" still another asked.

"Yes, I do."

"Well," he added, "he says in the paper today that you think drinkin' is a sin. Did you tell him to print that?"

"No," I answered.

They smiled at each other and nodded their heads in satisfaction. But I wiped the smiles off their faces when I added quickly, "But I said it."

There was a long silence while they looked at me as if I were demented. Then one of them stood up.

"Well, if that's the case," he said, "we've decided not to build the golf course." What he meant was that they had decided I wouldn't build their golf course.

I cannot understand the thinking of such people. I am certain that if they were drowning and I threw them a life preserver, they would not reject it just because I believe in God. I do not go around pinning people to walls and making them listen to me. Certainly, if they want help I try to give it to them from my own personal experiences. But I don't force myself on them unless they ask. Yet in this case they didn't want me to build their golf course because I didn't believe in drinking.

And, in connection with helping others, another thing I cannot understand is why so many ministers themselves are receiving psychiatric treatment, and why they send so many of those who come to them for help to see psychiatrists instead of raising an alcoholic from his own personal quagmire with their faith. To me, Jesus Christ is the psychiatrist and the healer.

Many people skid into the depths because they feel that they are below the level of public acceptance. God's wisdom can and will save them. For if they believe in the Bible, they will realize that they are as good as anyone else. It's right there in Romans 3:23:

"For all have sinned, and come short of the glory of God."

With Lloyd Mangrum at the P.G.A. National Golf Club in Dunedin, Fla., 1949. Spence is wearing the knickers his mother made for him when he was fifteen. Clearwater Sun, Fla.

5

For the drunkard and the glutton shall come to poverty: and drowsiness shall clothe a man with rags. *Proverbs 23:21*

A.A. and D.T.'s

My commitment to that rest home from which I escaped by knocking out the gate guard had been such a severe mental and nervous shock that I managed to keep myself straight for some time. I knew, however, that I was a man walking a tight-wire, and analyzed that the best way to stay out of further trouble was to keep busy physically.

It seemed like the answer to a prayer when right at this time I received an offer from a golf company to become its representative in seven eastern states. With headquarters in Washington, I was to visit country clubs throughout my territory, talking to golf professionals and selling equipment. Another of my duties was to set up showrooms at hotels in large cities where major tournaments were being played.

Eventually this latter phase of my duties took me to Pittsburgh, where the Dapper Dan tournament was being played. My old friend Kirby Higbe at this time was pitching for the Pittsburgh Pirates. He and his wife were living in nearby Homestead, Pennsylvania, and she was momentarily expecting a baby.

That Saturday Higbe pitched against the New York Giants and I went to the game with him. Going into the last inning he was leading and should have had the final out, when an infielder booted the ball for an error, which loaded the bases. Willard Marshall of the Giants then unloaded a home run which beat Higbe, and he was the hottest man I've ever seen. So mad that we both went out and got plastered.

Both Higbe's wife and I wound up in the same hospital. She to have her baby. And me because I came up with a ruptured cyst on my leg which had to be lanced.

"Man, that thing hurts," I told the doctor. "How about a little hooker?"

He handed me about four fingers in a water tumbler and I threw it down with a gusty sigh of relief.

"How do you feel now?" asked the doctor.

"How do I feel? Doc, now you can cut off both legs."

Sunday I lived through the tortures of the damned

with my hangover. Finally I called a bellboy and asked him to get me a bottle.

"It'll cost you $22.50," he told me.

Imagine, $22.50 for a $4 bottle of whiskey!

"Cheap at twice the price," I told him. So he got it for me and I knocked it off in less than an hour.

It didn't make much sense to Dottie. "Why is it you can't drink like ordinary people?" she asked with understandable impatience. "Most folks don't take a drink until after five o'clock and then they have dinner and they're all right."

"All right," I told her, "from now on I won't drink until five o'clock."

I really did try for a few days. But when you are in the shape into which I had quickly retrogressed, this was only a delaying tactic. As an example, one day I was at Reading, Pennsylvania, and the pro was purchasing a good-sized order of equipment, but all I could think of was that it was only four o'clock. So I turned up my watch an hour, as a sop to whatever conscience I had, and headed for the bar.

Shame bows my shoulders when I admit that I became so drunk that I wet the bed simply because I couldn't get up and make it to the bathroom. Tears dampened my pillow when I awoke and, filled with remorse and regret, realized what I had done. It was obvious to me that I couldn't live with whiskey and yet I felt that I couldn't live without it. I was on a vicious treadmill and there didn't seem to be any way to get off.

During the latter part of this frenzied year we went

to Chicago for a Professional Golf Association meeting, and once again I had drunk too much when Dottie and I boarded the train to go back to Columbia for a brief visit. I was in an upper berth and Dottie was in a lower just beneath me.

"Johnny," her voice floated up to me softly, "you should read this book."

She reached the book up to me. It was one in which Lillian Roth, a showgirl, told of her long battle against alcoholism and how Alcoholics Anonymous had helped her. Somewhere I had heard someone discussing the book and knew its general theme.

"I met her one time in Chicago or someplace," I whispered down to Dottie.

"Well, this girl had a problem, too," she said.

"I know about that A.A.," I retorted. "That group therapy stuff isn't for me."

Of course, Dottie was only clutching at any straw available in an effort to help me. Even though I knew this, and deep within myself raged and ranted at my weakness, it was typical of my thinking that I turned my resentment on her. Her suggestion filled me with cold anger, and when we arrived home I called a liquor store and had them fill a large refrigerator in my office at the house with beer.

For nineteen days I sat in my office drinking beer until you would have thought it was going to run out my ears. I emptied the refrigerator and had it refilled again and again. People called and I wouldn't answer the telephone. Finally my mother sent the minister to see me and he talked to me for an hour. I couldn't wait for him to leave so I could get back to drinking. He told me a lot of things, about how maybe I should see a psychiatrist, and that I shouldn't drink so much, as if I didn't already know that much, anyhow.

But he never told me that Jesus Christ was the answer to this thing, or that I should make a personal commitment to Jesus Christ, or that his grace was sufficient.

Read it yourself in Ephesians 2:8–9: "For by grace are ye saved through faith; and that not of yourselves: it is the gift of God:

"Not of works, lest any man should boast."

On the twentieth day I was on the point of committing suicide. Dottie had tried everything, to the point of constantly putting cold towels on my head and rubbing my back by the hour to try to get me to sleep. She had gone to the grocery store and I sat there, still drinking beer, wondering why I didn't just destroy myself. Why should I live, I asked myself, if I couldn't control my own life. Then I thought of the Roth book and went and found it in the bookcase. I skimmed through it and found and read the part about how A.A. had helped her. Maybe, I reasoned, they possibly could help me.

Looking in the telephone book, I found a listing for Alcoholics Anonymous. Twice I tried to call but both times the line was busy. Each time I went back and drank more beer, by this time finding it necessary to hold my nose because the odor sickened me. Finally I actually put a clothespin on my nose because I had the shakes so badly I needed both hands to keep the beer from spilling when I raised the glass to my mouth.

A third time I tried the A.A. number and this time a man's voice answered. I still wasn't quite sure that I wanted anything to do with them.

"Is this the place . . ." I hesitated and then started again. "Is this the place for people who have a drinking problem?"

"Do you have a drinking problem?" the man asked.

"Oh, no, not me," I replied. "I'm just asking for a friend. What are the dues and when do you meet?"

"We'll be glad to come out any time and help him," the voice told me.

"Oh, no, that's not necessary," I said hurriedly. "I just wanted information for this fellow. Forget it."

I hung up and went back for more beer. But I couldn't get that Roth book out of my mind. Dottie still hadn't returned from the grocery store so I went out finally and, taking the other car, drove to the A.A. address, stopped, then drove off again. I rode back and forth in front of the place a dozen times and, finally, having worked up enough courage, parked, and walked up to the door. It was opened by a friend of mine.

"Come in," he said with a smile. "We wondered how long it would take you to get here. We knew it was you who called, Johnny."

He and several others talked to me, telling me how they had been as bad as I looked and how, since going "on the wagon," they felt great. They told me they had 125 members and were having a meeting that night which I should attend. I said I would, and my friend rode home with me and stayed with me until it was time to return to the meeting.

Dottie was really thrilled that I had gone to A.A. "Johnny, it's truly a move in the right direction," she said.

When we went back to the meeting I met a lot of other friends and, realizing that they all had been in the same shape as I, I figured there was hope for me here. There was a picture of Christ on the wall, and I felt almost as if I were in a cathedral.

Then one man ruined it all for me, a fat, greasy-looking fellow who puffed his way up to the front of the room and surveyed the gathering with the eye of a man looking over the monkey house at the zoo. He had loose, wet lips. A cigar was clamped in the corner of his mouth and he never even bothered to take it out when he spoke in a guttural, condescending voice.

"My name's Cholly," he said. "I'm an alky. Been sober now for three years. I saved seven guys all by myself this year."

Forcing my eyes away from him, I stared at the picture of Jesus on the wall. The cigar smoke rose up in a thick, bluish cloud and blotted the picture from my sight. His voice rasped on and I cringed inside, feeling almost as if I were engaging in something obscene.

"You fellas have to do like I do. Give out those chips. Long as they carry that chip they're members in good standing. Glad to see we finally got our old friend Johnny Spence in here. Welcome aboard, Johnny. Now you're an ex-alky, too."

He laughed, his barrel belly shaking, and taking the cigar out of his mouth spat lustily into a corner of the room. I felt nauseated and even more disgusted with

him than I had been with myself. Instead of my having
been raised, Satan came into me through that man.
Gagging, I jumped up and walked out. Somewhere, and
I don't remember where, I bought a bottle and went
home. There I drank that whole bottle along with more
beer.

That night I almost died. There was a thunderstorm
which started about midnight. At 12:30 there was a
power failure and the lights went out. And right about
then I went into the d.t.'s. My teeth locked and I tried
to scream but couldn't. Strange things crawled all over
my flesh. I had delusions and hallucinations.

Dottie and my sister-in-law got me onto my bed, but
now the telephone was out of order, too. My sister-in-
law kept trying to hold me on the bed while Dottie
went out into that storm and brought back a doctor. He
gave me a needle that put me to sleep, and kept me
under sedation for several days until gradually I started
to eat again.

I was sober eight whole weeks this time. During this
period I had an idea that was to develop into a real
money-maker. The late Ed Dudley, then the president
of the P.G.A. and home pro at the Augusta National
Golf Club, where the Masters is held, had complained
to me that he had a rough time and lost money on his
shop every year during the tournament. Visiting pros,
of course, purchased items wholesale. Some of them
went off after the tournament ended and "forgot" to
pay even the wholesale price.

My idea was to start an open-air golf shop, in a tent
or trailer, away from the pro shop. Fully stocked with

all kinds of equipment and supplies, it was my theory
that spectators would drop by and, even if they didn't
buy anything, it would plant a sales seed for the future.
If I could set this up, with a commission of the gross
for me and a slice for the host professional, who would
be relieved of merchandising duties, I was certain that,
moving from tournament to tournament on the circuit,
it would be a solid financial success.

The first move had to be made in the direction of the
manufacturers, so Dottie and I went to New York to
commence our inquiries and make our sales pitch. We
stayed at the Astor Hotel and I met with various manufacturers who either were based in New York or were
in attendance at the Wykagyl Round Robin tournament
then underway at New Rochelle.

They didn't buy it. As a matter of fact, most of them
were dead set against it. I talked myself blue in the
face, but when I didn't seem to be getting anywhere I
finally threw up my hands and headed for the bar. It
was the same old story. On my way back to the hotel,
drunk and disconsolate, I stopped and picked up a
bottle of whiskey at a liquor store. When I awoke the
next morning I needed a drink as badly as I ever had
in my life, but my bottle was missing. Shaking all over,
I ransacked the room and finally grabbed the phone in
a rage and called the manager's office.

"You run a crooked hotel," I yelled. "I want somebody to find my jug or you'll pay through the nose."

Someone from the manager's office finally appeared
and tried to soothe me, but I wasn't having any. Then,
as I stormed around the room, he walked into the bath-

room and found my bottle where I had cached it behind the toilet. I wasn't the least bit embarrassed.

"Gimme that and get out," I said, tearing off the cork
with my teeth and taking a big slug right out of the
bottle. "Go on, get out."

He "got." But I know he must have thought I was
crazy.

With Dottie's help, however, I didn't go off on a
protracted bender. I had the lure of my idea to hold
onto and I drove ahead. When Sam Snead and Lloyd
Mangrum told me they liked the plan, we formed a
sales promotional organization, which I fronted. With
their help I finally got the manufacturers to go along
with my idea and we received a great deal of merchandise on consignment.

So it was that we launched the open-air golf shop in
April at the 1949 Masters in Augusta. We started with
a tent, but such was its instant success that eventually
we had to buy trailers to carry all of the equipment.
The biggest part of our sales was in small items such
as hats, seats, and umbrellas; but the manufacturers
paid us liberally merely to show and demonstrate their
equipment. Later we made a tie-up with an automobile
company which annually put Miss America under
contract. We parked the automobiles they gave us
conspicuously near our trailers and arranged Miss
America's television and personal appearances. Money,
in ever-increasing quantities, really started to roll in.

Putting this all together at the beginning kept me so
busy that, while occasionally I thought about taking a
drink, I kept so occupied I didn't seem to have time to

get around to it. It was hard work, driving from one tournament to another, setting up our shop for the public, giving everybody who stopped in the big hello, knocking down operations after the tournament ended, and hurrying on to the next site. By the fall, when the tour reached Grand Rapids, my nerves were starting to get the best of me.

Then, one evening, there was a banquet for the players. Dottie and I were sitting with Mangrum, Lawson Little, and their wives, when the waiter put a bottle of whiskey in front of every couple. Licking my lips, which suddenly were dust-dry, I knew if I didn't get out of there I was going to grab that bottle and take the first of too many gulps. Without saying anything to anybody, and leaving Dottie sitting right there with the others, I jumped up from the table and, walking out the front of the hotel, approached a cab driver.

"Do you know where Alcoholics Anonymous is?" I asked him.

"Yes, sir."

"Well," I said, leaping into the cab, "take me there as fast as you can."

"Yes, sir," he said emphatically.

But when we arrived, there was nobody at the place, so I told him to drive me back to the hotel. In the lobby I found a phone booth, looked up A.A. in the book, and dialed the number that was listed. The man who answered could tell by my voice that I was in trouble.

"Stay right there in the phone booth until I get there," he directed. "I'll know you."

After what seemed like hours, although it probably

was only a short period of time that I sat there shaking and sweating, there was a rap on the door of the booth. He was an elderly little man with pink cheeks and white hair. Together we went up to my room.

"You're going to be all right," he calmed me. "Let me tell you, Johnny, I know exactly what you're going through. I'm a doctor, and a good one, but liquor always seemed to get me. I've been up and down so often that I feel like a yo-yo. I'd get straight and then I'd fall off the wagon again. But you have to keep trying."

Talking to him calmed me down and I ordered up some coffee. While we were drinking it, Dottie arrived back at the room. The old gentleman left and I seemed to be all right again.

We went from there to Pittsburgh and Washington, but then I suddenly got the jitters again, took a beer, and less than two weeks after my meeting with the doctor I was dog-drunk. At least I knew one thing as far as A.A. and I were concerned: my instability was so tremendous that I was safe only when somebody was sitting there holding my hand. Then there is that chip which they give you to carry and which, in some mystic manner, is supposed to give you strength to resist your urge for a drink when you hold it in your hand. Somehow it never worked for me. And the mumbo-jumbo of breaking it when you fall and start drinking again is like something out of a voodoo ceremony.

Such as the time in Washington when I drunkenly called A.A.

"I'm drunk and I need help," I said.

"Did you break your chip?"

Imagine, did I break my chip? "No," I replied.

"Break it," he ordered.

I broke it by smashing it against the telephone, hung up, and went out for another drink.

Fortunately for my new operation, Washington was our last tournament that fall and nobody realized I had started drinking as heavily as I had, because we went back to Columbia. Almost as soon as we arrived, I met a friend who told me there was a rest home nearby which would "take care of me" for $200 a week plus "extras."

The thing to do, I reasoned, was to check in there and dry out before I went on another monumental bender. This I did, but after trying to rest in my room for a couple of hours I became so restless that I had to get out and talk to somebody. In the hall I met a man who turned out to be an Air Force colonel I had known. His breath reeked of whiskey.

"Say, Colonel, where did you get the liquor?" I asked.

"Man," he grinned, "you can get all of it you want. Of course, that's one of the 'extras' for which they charge you."

"Well, I have to get me some or go off my rocker," I admitted.

"Nothing to it," he told me, and then called a pretty nurse who was walking down the hall.

"Nurse," the colonel said to her, "Mr. Spence is upset about how he is being treated around here."

She was a pretty young girl, her uniform a fresh white and crisply starched, and she took my arm and gave it a little pinch.

"Why, Mr. Spence, what can I do for you?"

"I'll tell you what," I said. "If somebody doesn't get me a drink, I'm gonna knock down a few doors."

"There's no need for that," she told me. "I'll be right back."

She was, too, and with a bottle of whiskey.

This, I decided, was the greatest. All you wanted to drink, no necessity of winding up in the gutter, and a pretty girl to serve you if you had the money to pay for those "extras." I had it. So I stayed for two weeks, the doctor finally dried me out gradually, and I went home delighted with this new setup.

Yet it was a trap which in the long run could only make life more miserable for me. How much better things would have been, how much misery I would have been saved, if I had known, as it says in Proverbs 23:20:

"Be ye not among winebibbers . . ."

Spence and friend, Sam Snead (left),
at the Los Angeles Open, 1950.

Woe unto them that rise up early in the morning, that they may follow strong drink . . . *Isaiah 5:11*

Mixing "Medicine" and Whiskey

Early in 1950, before heading for the West Coast, where the pro golf tour was to open, I went to Detroit to sign a new and more lucrative contract with the automobile firm I was representing. Then we went on to Los Angeles, and I remember it well because it was Dottie's first airplane ride.

It was a happy period—destined to be rather brief, unfortunately—because I had dried out temporarily to make a good appearance in Detroit and vowed, as usual, that this time I was going to make it stick.

But then, as usual, the inevitable occurred. Our baggage was lost and, while waiting for it to be found, I started drinking in the airport. Dottie was frantic, fearing that I would go off on another tear. She was also apprehensive because if it became known that I was an alcoholic, our constantly growing income might be cut off.

I knew that I was about to go off the deep end again, and it so happened that I ran into a friend who was wrestling with the same problem.

"Johnny, there's a new real high-class place in South Carolina," he told me, mentioning a small town near home. "It's been taken over by two doctors and they do a good job."

So back we went. As soon as we landed, I sent Dottie home alone. I had, at this time, a new Lincoln. Next I bought a bottle of liquor and, drinking with one hand and driving 120 miles an hour with the other, started for this new rest home my friend had told me about. En route I stopped at several joints, met several marines I knew in one place, and wound up roaring drunk. But I finally did get to the rest home.

Still, I didn't know anything about this place, I reasoned, and I wasn't taking any chances on their being tough. So I cached six pints of liquor and some money in the trunk of the car, and hid the key to the trunk in one of my socks.

They were tough. For I was called into the office after a couple of days and the supervisor told me, "Spence, it's cold turkey for you now." That meant I wasn't going to get anything but would simply have to sweat out my withdrawal.

Johnny wasn't having any of that. I managed to sneak out to the car whenever things got real bad and down a half pint in one gulp. They couldn't figure out where I was getting the liquor. Then I just walked out and went to a place where I could buy beer. There I met a man who, after we had told each other our troubles, gave me a sly wink.

"Here, drop one of these in your beer," he said, reaching into his pocket and producing a bottle of pills.

"What are they?"

"Yellow jackets," he chuckled. "They got a real sting to 'em, too, friend."

They were, I discovered later, Nembutal. As he said, they had a real sting. I could hardly walk back to the rest home. There the doctor met me at the door.

"Spence," he said flatly, "we'd like you to leave. We're not doing you any good and you're upsetting everybody else around here."

So I gathered my few belongings, piled into the car, and thumbed my nose at the doctor as I drove out the gate. The first thing I did was to stop at a filling station and buy a case of beer, which I put on the seat beside me. Then, drinking as I drove, I tried to figure out what to do. There was only one answer. I went home.

Dottie wasn't in the house and I stumbled next door to my mother's. The only one there was an elderly colored lady who had taken care of me when I was a boy and my mother happened to be away. Soon after I went back to my house, she knocked on the door and came in at my bidding. She didn't have to be told that I was in bad shape, and there was deep concern in her voice.

"Mr. Johnny, you know God loves you. Nobody wants to see you suffering like this."

I had thrown myself down on a couch. Then, bless her heart, she kneeled down beside me and for several hours rubbed my back and neck soothingly, softly singing hymns all the while, until I fell asleep.

The next day, of course, I made another solemn vow to quit. It was easy. I had made the same vow a thousand times, and practice makes perfect. My good resolution did last awhile. I played a great deal of golf and began to feel truly fit again.

But then came a Saturday when I made a hole in one. The next day, a Sunday when I should have been in church but refused to go with Mother and Dottie, I scored another hole in one. Of course I had to celebrate but, surprisingly enough for me, I held it within some sort of bounds.

It was too good to last. My thirst had been unleashed again, and the next week it smashed the dyke of my temporary self-restraint when I went to Fort Bragg to play in a tournament as a partner to three officers who were friends of mine.

Although I had managed to hold a checkrein of sorts on my drinking, I showed up with a hangover and played poorly with a 37 on the first nine holes. Just before we started the back nine, one of the officers' wives brought out some cold beer. I downed four bottles and carried more with me out onto the course. By now I was feeling exhilarated and I shot a 32 on the back nine for a 69.

There was a smashup party that night at which I insulted my host and hostess and wound up spending the night in the officers' club bar. The next day, still higher than a Georgia pine, I shot a 66 and won the tournament. Now this must be proof, I exonerated myself, that drinking can't hurt you. So I wound up getting really blasted.

This was the story of that whole year: drinking as secretly as possible, fighting to straighten myself out, and somehow or other, mostly through Dottie's help, managing to do my job and seeing it become increasingly more lucrative. Yet, as we neared the end of the tour, I felt certain that I wasn't going to be able to continue deceiving the world very much longer.

When the tour ended in the fall, I renewed my vow that I was going to lick this thing and returned once more to the rest home in Carolina where I knew I could get liquor. But so worried was I about my job and my rising income that this time I went there determined to beat the bottle.

"I don't want any liquor," I told the head nurse. "I've got to get back on the job and I mean I can't have any liquor."

She could see that I was in frightful shape, my nerves screaming and my whole being in a tremendous state of agitation. So after I got in bed she came in with a needle and gave me a shot of Pentothal in the left arm.

Placing a cold cloth on my head, she sat on the edge of the bed talking to me and rubbing my hands. In a few moments the nausea which had been making me ill for days was gone and I was asleep.

"I don't know what you did, but I sure do thank you," I told her the next morning.

"You're so underfed, you ought to have some glucose."

I begged off, telling her that Dottie was coming to pick me up.

"Well, you ought to take something," she admonished me.

"All I need," I suggested, "is something to calm me down and make me sleep."

"Maybe I've got just the thing," the nurse told me, leaving. She returned with a two-ounce bottle which she said was elixir of Nembutal. "Just take a teaspoonful of this in some water and you'll sleep."

That night I didn't take it, feeling that I might be all right. I managed to sleep fitfully, but the next night when Dottie and I were on the road I came up with the shakes, and a teaspoonful in water, as she had promised, relaxed me and put me to sleep.

As the spring of 1951 rolled around I was so busy working that, managing to stay away from liquor, I didn't need anything. Often it was a bitter battle, but with Dottie's help I stayed on the straight and narrow and plunged myself into the hectic business of running the open-air golf shop. It held me in the public eye and I realized how fortunate I had been to keep my weakness a secret.

We motored up through the East, to the United States Open at Oakland Hills in Birmingham, Michigan, and down to Washington. Leaving Washington I made the wrong turn and went a hundred miles out of the way. To add to my aggravation, going up a mountain road the automobile overheated and I burned up the motor, nearly jackknifing the trailer. A state trooper appeared and told me I'd have to clear the road, and I had a heated argument with him.

Dottie calmed me down but it was a period when everything seemed to be going wrong. During the P.G.A. championship at Oakmont Country Club, outside of Pittsburgh, there was a violent storm and we worked practically all night to save the large array of merchandise displayed in our tent.

As a Christian, I know now that a man can rid himself of these aggravations and anxieties through supplication and thanksgiving. Consider the solace in Philippians 4:6-7:

"Be careful for nothing; but in every thing by prayer and supplication with thanksgiving let your requests be made known unto God.

"And the peace of God, which passeth all understanding, shall keep your hearts and minds through Christ Jesus."

Yet on the day the P.G.A. ended, with my nerves as taut as the strings on a guitar, some friends brought a case of beer to the trailer and the smell was too much for me in my state of tension. I only had a few. But the next day when we finished cleaning up the premises and pulled away from the club, I already had drunk a

dozen beers and insisted on stopping at a bar. This led
to stops at others. Finally I bought a fifth of whiskey,
and by the time we stopped for the night at a motel in
Carlisle I was soddenly inert.

Morning brought remorse and embarrassment, but
not enough to keep me from having "just a few to
straighten me out." I did force myself to shape up because we had to go into New York for a business conference with our automobile sponsors. Once that had
been taken care of, we headed home—only to meet some
friends in Myrtle Beach, South Carolina, and now I
went on a bender that lasted almost three weeks.

Dottie was finally able to pack me off home and this
time she took me to the rest home, which seemingly
had become my home away from home. My long-suffering wife must have laid down a bit of law, although
I don't remember very much, for they gave me a shot
and when I awoke my arm was strapped to a board and
I was being given glucose intravenously. There wasn't
any liquor. So I started to eat and, such was the strength
of my constitution, within a week I was out and feeling
fine again.

By now we were earning in the rather exclusive
neighborhood of $5,000 a week and, lecturing myself
sternly, I went "on the wagon" for several months. Our
holidays were the brightest in years, and the finest gift
of all to my family was that I remained sober.

That spring was one of the happiest we had known
in years, for we made all of the California tournaments
and I steadfastly shunned the bottle. We did a tele-
vised golf show in San Antonio with Julius Boros, Doug

Ford, and Jimmy Turnesa, and we all thought it was hilarious when Boros hit the camera with a ball and broke up the show. I was, for some reason I still can't fathom, seemingly as relaxed as a kitten.

But slowly, inexorably, it was catching up with me. By the time we reached the Masters my pressure valve was beginning to show signs of blowing, and our task there that week was complicated by incessant rain. The tournament ended on Sunday night, and an acquaintance who stopped by to pass the time of day gave me the excuse I needed.

"Man, you look like a wreck. Let's have a drink."

"I haven't had a drink in months," I replied.

"Well, relax, man. That's exactly what you need."

I wound up back in the rest home for ten days. "I need some sleep," I told the doctor. "Quick."

"That's easy," he said, returning with a large needle. He jabbed me with it and I was out like a light.

The next day I asked for a bottle of whiskey. It was produced immediately; but they had started cutting the liquor, undoubtedly to increase their already considerable profits, so I sent out for my booze.

Now I was on both medication and drink, a lethal combination, and I knew I had to get off it. But this is easier said than done. On this occasion I had a private nurse and I figured that the elixir of Nembutal would turn the trick as it had before.

"The last time I was here," I told her, "they gave me a little bottle of . . ."

"I know," she smiled, "but you have to know how to use it."

She returned with the Nembutal and gave me less than a teaspoonful in a glass of water. It acted like a superdrink of whiskey because I felt wonderful immediately. I was, I realized, as high as a kite. This wasn't medicine. What we were having was a "smoker" in pajamas.

Using Nembutal this way, I analyzed, I could be the life of the party without smelling of whiskey. And when things got too bad I could always increase the dosage and get a good night's sleep.

Leaving the rest home, I went to a doctor who knew I was an alcoholic.

"Doc," I kidded him, "this stuff works great. Why don't you let me be your exclusive distributor? We can make a fortune."

He laughed and gave me several prescriptions for elixir of Nembutal in both tablet and liquid form.

"Only use these occasionally to keep yourself from getting high-strung," he advised.

What a dope, I thought. He's given me the means to stay high without my ever having to smell of alcohol.

The prescriptions lasted me until August, when I was in Chicago, and my nerves were getting the best of me again. There I took my last one to a drugstore and returning to the hotel accidentally dropped it, cursing my luck as it smashed on the floor of the lobby of the hotel. Stripping off the label, to which a piece of glass still was attached, I went back to the drugstore and told the pharmacist what had happened.

"I'll let you have more, but you'll have to get the prescription sent to me," he said.

I wired the doctor at home so that the pharmacist wouldn't get into trouble, went back to the hotel, took a big jolt of Nembutal, and slept like an infant. But now I realized how precious this stuff was to me. I could go to a party, never take a drink but go to the men's room and take a shot of Nembutal, and have more fun than any of them.

It became so important to me that I would fly home just to get new prescriptions from the doctor and then fly back to wherever we happened to be running our open-air golf shop. But this wasn't always possible. Our automobile contract had grown into a plump promotional pie with every prospect of getting bigger. At the Fort Wayne Open we made a documentary film in color, and one of the scenes which never got into the finished product was when the late Porky Oliver, conducting a clinic, hit a shot which sailed right through the window of one of those portable outhouses, and a man inside ran out in terror with his trousers still at half-mast.

From there I went to a meeting with the auto firm's agency at a country club in Atlanta. Everything looked rosy because I had my elixir, and just before the meeting I took my "medicine." Then somebody produced a fifth of liquor and poured a big straight shot for me.

That's all I remember about that evening. Mixing my "medicine" and whiskey was a deadly combination. Ed Dudley, the pro at the Augusta National, had driven to Atlanta with me, along with his wife, Ruth, and Dottie. He finally got me under a shower and gradually I began to regain my senses.

"Where am I?" I asked him, even more sick with embarrassment as I vomited in the shower. "What happened?"

Ed helped me get dressed, and as we walked out through the locker room I saw a half-empty bottle of warm, stale beer sitting on a table filled with dirty glasses. I snatched it up and drank it down.

The next morning, Dottie and Ruth drove Ed's car while Ed and I followed in my brand-new automobile that I had picked up in Atlanta. While they drove on ahead, we checked off the dry counties and stopped to get a drink wherever we could. Finally I fell asleep while Ed drove on into Augusta and stopped in front of his son-in-law's house for a brief visit, leaving me to sleep a bit more in the car. He also left the keys in the ignition.

While he was gone I awoke, barely realizing where I was, and it nagged at the back of my mind that I was supposed to meet Dottie in Columbia. I didn't give Ed a thought but just drove off. The road was blurred and kept dancing in front of my eyes, so I stopped for a few beers and then headed out the four-lane highway to Aiken. I was so confused that I hardly knew where I was going, yet somehow I found my way to Highway 215.

About eight miles outside of Aiken there is a slight dip in the road, and a curve. Weaving my way along this road that wouldn't hold still, I took the curve on the wrong side and suddenly, right in front of me, there loomed a tractor-trailer truck which looked as gigantic as Mohammed's mountain. Mohammed and the mountain came to each other, hit head on, and my world was blotted out in a blinding flash accompanied by the wail of tortured metal. I didn't know until weeks later what had happened, how the force of the crash caused $8,000 worth of damage to the truck and made a total wreck of my new car, which had little more than 200 miles on the speedometer.

Actually, a piece of the steering wheel pierced the right side of my abdomen and one lung; five of my teeth were sheared off, my left hand was broken, and my entire body was covered with cuts and bruises.

When the truck sent my car careening off the highway in a mass of twisted metal, the door snapped open and I was flung seventy feet. No one knew I was there until a young boy ran up and told those who stopped, "There's a man lying over there in that ditch."

How prophetic that in Matthew 24:40 it says: "Then shall two be in the field; the one shall be taken, and the other left."

They took me to a hospital in Aiken where the doctor in the emergency room, an old golfing friend of mine, took one look at me and said, "He must be dead."

Later I was transferred to a hospital in Columbia, and three weeks after that, mostly skin and bone but still able to navigate, I went home. Within a month, thanks to that cast-iron and piano-wire constitution which already had sustained so much, I boarded a plane for Chicago to attend the Professional Golfers Association meeting. I still needed codeine tablets to check the pain of my injuries, but I also was well equipped with a pocketful of Nembutal.

It was at this meeting that we cemented a deal for my automobile sponsor to become a co-sponsor of the International Jaycees golf championship. My automobile company was also employing Miss America in various projects, and we decided to use her in promoting the tournament. The first one was held at the University of Michigan golf course in Ann Arbor in August of 1953, and a fine young man named Johnny Pott, who since has gained fame on the professional tour, captured the driving championship. One of the brightest spots was the appearance of our Miss America, Neva Jane Langley, of Macon, Georgia.

Don Moomaw, an All American football star at U.C.L.A. and a divinity student, came to me at that tournament and asked me to get him a date with Neva Jane. During the course of our conversation he said that he planned to refuse to play professional football in the United States but would go to Canada, where he would not have to play on Sunday. I tried to talk him out of it on the grounds that he would make more money in the United States but he was adamant, a solid Christian young man.

Ten years later, in the spring of 1963, I was asked to appear at Greenville, Texas, in a crusade called Athletes for Christ. Don Moomaw, by this time an ordained Presbyterian minister, met me and drove me to the meeting.

"Billy Graham told me about you," he said, "but I couldn't place you."

"I'm the fellow who tried to talk you out of not playing football on Sundays in the United States," I explained.

"Now I remember," he smiled. "But I'm glad to say it didn't do you any good."

At that first International Jaycee tournament, a seventeen-year-old from Atlanta ended in a tie for the championship on Saturday. His name was Jimmy Raines, and he refused to compete in a playoff on Sunday. I rushed over to talk to him.

"I'm sorry, Mr. Spence," he explained, "but I'm going to be a preacher and Sunday belongs to the Lord. I just can't play."

This was a job for a supersalesman, and Spence was the man to fill the bill.

"Jimmy," I confided with my arm around his shoulders, "I wouldn't want you to play golf on Sunday for all the money in the world. But these fine folks brought all you boys here from all over the country and a lot of other places, and the whole world is waiting for the end of this tournament. This other boy wants to get home and he figures he's going to beat you tomorrow. You owe it to all of us to see this thing through, no matter what the sacrifice is personally, and to uphold the honor of the South. You have a commitment, son, and you're honor bound to live up to it."

Well, the upshot was that Jimmy played as a result of my persuasion. Not only that, he beat the pants off the other boy.

Ten years later, as in the case of Moomaw, I met Jimmy Raines when he was a minister traveling on a campus crusade. Just a few days earlier, he told me, he had had a call late at night from one of the nation's outstanding nuclear physicists who was desperately fighting the bottle, which is added evidence that alcoholism can strike at any level. Jimmy, the boy who had listened to me a decade earlier, had carried faith to that poor soul.

But that day in 1953 when young Jimmy Raines won the first International Jaycee tournament in a Sunday playoff, I figured that I had spent a full week surrounded by a collection of nuts.

At the presentation ceremonies I ended the proceedings by saying, "God bless you all."

When I said it I was a little high from a dose of my "medicine" and hardly knew what was really going on. I don't know why I said it. All I can say is that it just popped out. There was a lot of money at stake and another jag in the offing. I was a modern Ahab who needed no Jezebel, for, as it is recorded in I Kings 21:26:

"And he did very abominably in following idols . . ."

President-elect Dwight D. Eisenhower at Augusta National Golf Course, hours after 1952 election returns, and pro Ed Dudley, friend of Spence and the general.

7

My days are swifter than a weaver's shuttle, and are spent without hope. *Job 7:6*

A Dead-end Road

There are occasional kind thoughts and pleasant instances of fine people and steadfast loyalties no matter how venomous life may have been at the moment for an individual.

Several years earlier I had been approached by a young pro named Art Wall, who, in a remarkably gentle fashion, asked me if I could help him to get on the staff of a shoe company which was among the many firms my traveling pro shop represented. Wall had been on the tour a couple of years without winning a tournament.

"I'll definitely keep you in mind," I told him, and, as was our custom with young pros, presented him with a couple of pairs of golf shoes.

Finally, he won his first tournament in 1953 at Fort Wayne by beating Cary Middlecoff in a playoff and, when he came off the course, I approached him.

"We'd like to have you with our shoe company," I said.

"Johnny Spence gave me shoes when nobody else paid me any attention," he said. "I'll never use anybody else's shoes but those of his company."

"But I am Johnny Spence," I told him, somewhat taken aback.

Only then did I realize how greatly the accident and the life I had been leading had altered my appearance.

Despite this shock, I remained on that same deadly treadmill. I took Miss America to the Celebrities Tournament at Washington and arranged a television show at Griffith Stadium with her, Sam Snead, trick-shot artist Paul Hahn, and Lew Worsham, among others. This was on a Wednesday, because the tournament was to commence the following day, but all of a sudden, as we arrived at the park, I felt as if my head were going to explode. My nerve ends were screaming and my heart pounded as if I were going to die on the spot.

"Take care of Neva Jane," I ordered a virtual stranger.

Then I rushed from the stadium to a nearby bar and ordered a double Scotch. My hands were shaking so violently that I could hardly raise the drink but had to bend over and practically suck it out of the glass. I

threw another double down on top of it before the first
one could bounce up, and fled to the men's room.
Frantically dousing my head with cold water, I sat on
a toilet with the door bolted until the liquor could take
effect, fighting all the while to hold it down.

Those two drinks made me a new man. Then the new
man had to have a few more. Soon I was back on my
feet.

There was a dinner that night at which I was supposed to sing while Neva Jane accompanied on the
piano, her specialty in winning the Miss America con-
test; Snead was to play the trumpet. Everything was
going along fine until Dugan Aycock, a golf professional
from North Carolina and a long-time friend of mine,
leaned across the table and advised me, "You're on
next."

In an instant I, Johnny Spence, supersalesman and a
glib man who loved the limelight, was scared speechless. The liquor had worn off and, with a premature
hangover setting in, I had plummeted to the mental
depths. Without a word I rose from the table, left
Dottie sitting there, and sneaked out a side door to find
a place where I could take some "medicine." Once
again I knew utter shame and total embarrassment. The
more I took, the more I required.

Soon I was so drunk, between alcohol and doses of
Nembutal, that I knew I had to disappear so that no
one would become suspicious.

I abandoned Dottie and the trailer and, taking a taxi-
cab to the airport, flew home and rushed to my haven,
that rest home where I could get all the care and sham

solicitude I needed simply because I could pay the price. I knew that Dottie could take care of things and would make my excuses—she had had so much experience at this.

This time I remained more than three weeks. The reason was that now there was a new nurse with marvelous understanding. She introduced me to the final step—Demerol, a morphine narcotic. This was really wild. One shot and you became a giant who held the world in the hollow of his hand. It is the stuff of which incest, adultery and worse are fashioned. The stuff that produces the deadliest of the deadly habits—the narcotics kick.

After a week I noticed that I wasn't getting quite so high, but my nurse, who wouldn't even have a drink with me, seemed to be walking on clouds. The next time she arrived to give me a needle I watched closely. Then the reason became obvious. She deftly slipped the needle into my arm and pressed the plunger. But not all the way. Then, pretending not to be watching, I saw her hold the needle down at her side and quickly plunge the needle into her thigh right through her white uniform. She was using half of the shot for which I was paying through the nose.

Rearing up in bed, I twisted her wrist and began to berate her. She turned whiter than her uniform.

"Please, Johnny," she pleaded desperately, "don't report me. I'm sorry and it won't happen again. But I have to have it, too."

I fell back limply, feeling sorry for her. She was, after all, in worse straits than I, because at least I could afford it, or thought I could. Besides, I reasoned, as my private nurse she was being extremely "nice" to me. It had become, as you might gather, that kind of a place.

Meanwhile, though I realized the added hazards of staying on morphine, I still had that old idiotic feeling, despite my repeated failures, that I could conquer any habit. Other lost souls who were there bolstered my insane confidence.

"You can get your own needle, and any doctor you know will let you have what you need," confided an attorney who was one of my fellow patients. "There's no use in dying."

No use at all. But, I found out later, he did die of it.

Still, I was able to locate a doctor who was liberal with his Demerol prescriptions and, to facilitate matters, I bought my own syringe. He also put me on another sedative called Tuinal. With these I could take two in thirty minutes and get along fine if the party didn't last too long. After that I started to lose my edge. So I began taking a double dose and I still was making more noise at the end of a party than the worst drunk who happened to be there.

Shortly after this, I had to go to New York for another business conference, and when it was over we wound up in the Stork Club. I had taken some of my "medicine" and after I started drinking on top of it I suffered another blackout. Dottie took care of getting us on a plane to Atlanta but, once there, we couldn't obtain a continuing reservation to Columbia.

"I don't know what to do," Dottie fretted.

"Buy a plane," I told her.

We settled my grandiose ideas by renting a private plane, and a few hours later I was back in the rest home, where diminishing doses of Demerol and sedatives again straightened me out temporarily so that I could pick up the tour at Miami.

I was carrying my own syringe and a pocketful of prescriptions when I went to the West Coast for the start of the 1954 tour, and gradually made myself kick the habit with more suffering than I can ever hope to explain. Most addicts cannot mix liquor and narcotics. It's one or the other. With me, I'd boot the habit but then start thinking about alcohol, and it was a vicious cycle.

By the time we got back to Augusta for the Masters, without admitting it in my inner mind I was planning to fall off the wagon with the most resounding crash in liquid history. By this time we had gone from one trailer to two trailers and finally to a giant tent. Feeling the storm brewing inside me, I obtained some elixir to settle my nerves.

The night the tournament ended, with Sam Snead and Ben Hogan tied, Dottie and I had dinner with Sam. Snead asked me if I had heard what the odds were, so I called a bookmaker in New York and found that Hogan was a three-to-one favorite. I called Greenbrier, where Snead is pro in the summer, and some friends of his came running with a satchel full of money to bet on him. I put up a large chunk of money on him, too.

This, of course, gave my weak will power the chance it wanted. Snead and Hogan were locked in a real eye-to-eye battle and when they came to the ninth hole I

couldn't stand it any longer but went to the bar and
started drinking doubles. I stayed there drinking doubles until the match ended with Sam winning by one
shot. Now the celebration of Sam's victory, and the
winning of my very profitable wager, became my excuse to keep right on going.

Three days later I had a caddy drive me to a new
rest home I had heard about. But caution long since had
been inbred, so again I resorted to the old stratagem of
hiding the key to my car in my sock. It was a wise pre-
caution. The supervisor was a fellow I had thrown out
of my club, and he proved his long-held dislike when I
was rash enough to tell him that his liquor was watered
and his drugs had been cut.

"I had a call from your family and they tell me I've
got to straighten you out," he snapped at me. "You're in
my hands, Spence, and I'm gonna make it a cold turkey
deal for you."

Spence wasn't having any. They had taken away my
clothes but I had hidden the key to my car in a box of
tissues. At the first opportunity, I sneaked out in my pajamas, crawled through a series of hedges, and jumped
into my car and sped off.

On the way home I stopped and called the house.
My Aunt Dolly answered the telephone. She knew
better than to fuss with me when I was in a state such
as this.

"Just make sure my needle's there and nobody has
thrown it out or hidden it," I snarled.

Arriving home, I walked upstairs, loaded the syringe
with some Demerol I had cached in my bedroom,

needled my own arm, and went soundly to sleep.

Then followed a period in which I kept myself on Demerol and Tuinal, a capsuled sedative. Together it was a deadly combination. One small Tuinal along with a shot of Demerol and you're in the twilight zone. I could really float for three or four hours, but when it died off I had to have more ready or nearly go out of my mind. Gradually I increased the dosage until I was using this combination five or six times in a row. It would, I knew, kill me sooner or later, so once again I gradually diminished the doses and forced my own withdrawal to the point where I could get along primarily on sedatives alone.

Our Miss America by this time was Evelyn Margaret Ay of Ephrata, Pennsylvania, and I was spurred to get myself back in some sort of shape because I had to take her to Albuquerque for a tournament appearance. Outwardly I appeared to be drawn from what I described to anybody who cared to listen as "overwork." Inwardly, I was a bundle of flaming nerve ends.

The night we arrived in Albuquerque, Dottie, Evelyn Margaret, Gene Sarazen and I went up into the mountains to one of our favorite restaurants. I couldn't eat for wondering how I could walk out, get down the mountain and take some "medicine," which, somehow or other, I had left in the hotel. The whole evening was a nightmare.

From Albuquerque I had to go to Los Angeles on business, but I ran out of both sedatives and drugs, and I just got up and walked off the plane at Phoenix to look for an understanding doctor. To make things worse, my ears were paining me from the altitude. For the first time in a long while I was hungry and I stopped in a restaurant to eat. Sitting on my table were two empty martini glasses with the olives still in them. While waiting for the waitress I reached into the glasses and ate the olives. Many, many martinis later I boarded a plane and went on to Los Angeles.

There the roof fell in on me. I couldn't bring myself to go to the business meeting which Joe Kirkwood Jr. had set up to consider a golf script for television. My long-suffering Dottie finally called Alcoholics Anonymous, but there was no one there available to come see me.

"Call a doctor," she was told.

Earlier, we had left our car in Chicago so we bought tickets to go back there and pick it up. At that time it was a six-hour trip. That was too long to be without whiskey but even in my highly agitated state, my cunning sharpened by my distress, I was fearful that they might put me off the airplane if I started drinking from a bottle. The thought nagged me so that I went to a drugstore and purchased seven three-ounce bottles and filled them from several quarts I had bought, my trembling hands spilling more in the process than I got into the little bottles. What I planned was to ration myself to one three-ounce shot every hour. In this way, after bracing myself with the remainder of what was in the quarts, I figured I could get through the trip without going right through the roof of the plane.

By the time we landed in Chicago, however, I had long since drunk all my whiskey and I needed more. As the cab driver drove us into the city, I spotted a liquor store on the opposite side of the street.

"Pull over there so I can get a bottle," I ordered.

"Can't make a U turn."

"Man," I snarled, reaching over and grabbing him by the collar, "if you don't I'm going to plumb beat you to death."

He took one look at me, turned the car, and stopped in front of the liquor store.

Dottie called A.A. again when we reached the hotel, but once more no one was available. Nor did she have any success reaching a doctor. Finally she did get a chiropractor who gave me a long rubdown, but I kept getting worse, so we left the car in Chicago, later sending a man from Columbia to get it, and caught a plane to Atlanta. I obtained tranquilizers there. By now, it seemed, I never got to my own house. It was off the plane and back to the rest home for a week.

That was all the time I could spare because I had to be in Cincinnati for an important meeting. No plane was available so I had to drive to Atlanta to take a train, racing against time. I happened to meet Ernie White, who had pitched for the St. Louis Cardinals and the Boston Braves and managed the Columbia baseball team, and he drove me to the train. They were just about to close the gates when we got there, with me in a sweating panic, and when I got into my roomette I was shaking like a tree in a hurricane. When the train stopped at Knoxville I asked the porter if there was any place to get a drink of liquor.

"No, sir," he shook his head, "this here is dry territory."

We had a half-hour layover so I raced uptown in a
cab, kept it waiting while I drank a half-dozen quick
beers, and took twenty cans of beer back to the train
with me and had the porter put them in an ice bucket.
Then I started rationing them so they'd last until I
arrived in Cincinnati.

Finally there, I reached my hotel, but that's as far as
I got. Sending out for whiskey, I told the operator that
if there were any calls she was to say I hadn't arrived.
Grimly I poured whiskey into myself, trying to kill the
craving that gnawed inside of me.

But by now the whiskey wasn't doing me any good.
Even in my desperation I was shocked to realize that I
had reached the point where nothing would do but
morphine.

It was out of the question to face the sponsors. Getting more whiskey, simply because I felt it was better
than nothing, I took a taxi right back to the airport and
flew straight to South Carolina and my rest home.

My usual private nurse greeted me with a satisfied
smile. "I knew that when the moon turned you'd be
back."

I was there three weeks this time.

Out once again, I cemented my lines of supply. It
was, I reasoned, the only way in which I could carry
on. The holidays were cheerless for us, because Dottie
and Mother knew full well what I was going through,
and I was glad to leave for the West Coast to rid my-

self of the compassion and misery which showed in my
family's eyes.

As long as I had Demerol and Tuinal, however, I was
still the life of the party. At one such affair in San Antonio I sat with Kyle Rote of the New York football
Giants and we drank nothing but soft drinks. All I had
to do was slip into the men's room and take a pill
and I was higher than anybody in the place, although
Rote didn't know this.

We were laughing it up when a drunk walked over
to us and demanded, "What are you guys, sneak
drinkers? You sit there drinking that soft stuff and you
can't be having this much fun on that hogwash."

"Don't you know the secret?" I asked him in a stage
whisper. "Look, all you do is put salt in this stuff and
it'll make you drunker than a coot."

The guy walked away and came back with a soft
drink. Picking up the salt shaker, he sprinkled salt gen-
erously into the soft drink. When he took a gulp, his
eyes lighted up.

"Man, that's a terrific drink," he yowled. "You guys
ought to get a patent on it. I can feel the kick in it. This
is wonderful."

We almost died laughing at the sucker.

With my "medicine" cabinet being rapidly depleted,
I was relieved when it came time to head for Augusta
and the Masters. Dottie hadn't arrived there yet and
Ed Dudley got me an apartment in town. Through two
doctors, one of whom is now an addict confined to
the government hospital at Lexington, Kentucky, I obtained Demerol in tablet form, the first I had seen.

They were easier to take than jabbing yourself with a needle.

Right after I started taking them, and undoubtedly consuming too many, I broke out in an ugly red rash which threatened to spread all over my body. Dudley called a doctor, who took one look into my eyes and told me, "You're on drugs and you've been taking too much." He said that he wouldn't treat me.

"Please, Doc," Dudley stopped him. "Take care of Johnny. He's my boy."

The doctor gave me some valid medicine and warned me to cut down on the drugs. I did, as much as I could, and the rash started to disappear. It had given me quite a scare, so I kept cutting down until again my hungry nerve ends seemed to be jutting right through my skin.

On the night the Masters ended, Ed and I had to wait for some people who were going to dinner with us. We started drinking beer, then switched to whiskey. To a system loaded with drugs this was dynamite. Without even telling her, I left Dottie to clean up the loose ends and headed straight back to the rest home.

Diabolical as such a place is, it was strange what a sense of relief surged over me whenever I reached there. These people, I felt, understood me. And here I wasn't an outcast who had to hang his head in shame, but only another one of "the boys."

When I arrived I was told that my former nurse had left, probably to take a real cure herself someplace where they were serious about helping addicts. My new nurse was a hefty blond German girl I had seen several times before, once when a patient slapped her and she hauled off and knocked him flat with one punch. She took good care of me immediately.

That night we had a real "pajama smoker." Most of about a dozen of us there were high on morphine, including a robust, black-haired man I shall call Harry Miller, who stood about six feet two inches tall. I had seen him there before, too, noticing him primarily because he had long spatulate fingers with broad, strong fingernails that made me think of razors. He had, someone told me, been a commando during the war, and he looked every bit the part.

Let me say right here that a man who is high on drugs will do things that a person intoxicated on liquor wouldn't even begin to think of doing. Anyhow, we were floating around the room, hooting and hollering and just "enjoying" ourselves, when somebody began to play the piano and several of us began to sing. Even now what happened is still not clear in all its details to me, but I know I thought of harmonizing with someone. I happened to be standing close to Miller so in sheer camaraderie I threw my arm around his shoulder. It was as if I had triggered a bomb. He whirled and backhanded me with the flat edge of his left hand and I felt as if I had been blackjacked. Then that shovel-sized right hand flashed into my face like an iron claw, and indescribable pain exploded in my head as his knife-like nails gouged into my right eye.

He plucked out my eye as if it were a grape.

Reeling back, I put a hand to my face. I could feel the eye floating loose on my cheek in a cascade of blood. Then, half blinded, I went absolutely crazy.

Roaring with rage and pain, I picked up a heavy metal ashtray standard and went for him. I meant to kill him on the spot and he knew it, for he whirled, ran toward a large French window, and sent glass and frame flying as he leaped right through it out into the night.

I wasn't ten feet behind him as I, too, dived head first through the shattered window. Outside, under the window, there were several large holly bushes. He had cleared them and fallen down in landing. I could hear him panting heavily as he leaped to his feet and ran off into the darkness. I landed square in the middle of the holly, shredding my pajamas while the holly thorns sent their needles raking across my body. He had disappeared by the time I managed to lunge free of the holly bushes. I took a few tottering steps and collapsed on the lawn.

Within a few seconds the powerful German nurse was beside me. Leaning over, she picked me up as if I were a child and carried me back into the house. Right in the foyer she laid me down on the floor and said into my ear, "Lie still, honey, or you'll bleed to death."

I tried to struggle erect. All I could think of was finding Miller and beating him to death. But she was stronger than I, and she pinned me to the floor while she ordered another nurse to bring a paraldehyde needle. When it came she snatched it and gave me the shot in the thigh, right through my tattered pajamas.

Numbly I lay there, staring through my one good eye at the gore spattered on her white uniform as she kneeled beside me, holding me down by the shoulders. The blood and the sight of my eye lying out on my cheek had sobered everybody, and they stood there looking down on me in a silent circle until the doctor arrived.

They didn't move me. As I lay there on the floor, the doctor, too, kneeled beside me and went to work. The lower lid had been torn wide open and, somehow or other, he placed the eye back in its socket and sewed up the lid. Then I was taken to a hospital.

For thirteen long weeks I lay in that hospital bed while they worked to keep from removing the eye completely. Thirteen weeks in which I plotted various methods of killing Harry Miller, and in which time they saved the eye although its vision was gone forever.

I decided, at long last, that I was going to find him, walk right up to him, and blow him in half with a double-barreled shotgun.

I tried. I found out where he lived and that he ran a store. For weeks I sat in front of his store by day and in front of his house by night with a loaded shotgun beside me, waiting for him to appear. But, I found out later, Miller had fled the state and didn't return for more than a year.

There is no question in my mind but that I would have killed him in cold blood and without a twinge of remorse. I believe that a divine power prevented me from exacting retribution. No, I know that is what happened. I am convinced when I read II Corinthians 12:9: "And he said unto me, My grace is sufficient for thee: for my strength is made perfect in weakness. Most gladly therefore will I rather glory in my infirmities, that the power of Christ may rest upon me."

God saved my life and saved me from killing another human being. Of this I am certain.

That summer I got through life on drugs alone and, being in constant pain from the slowly healing eye, had medical as well as moral justification. If ever there had been a question in my mind, I knew without any shadow of a doubt now that I was completely hooked. I wouldn't admit it, but I was rolling swiftly down the final hill of a dead-end road.

Desperately I tried to pull together the threads of my lucrative business, but they were vanishing with the inexorable steadiness of an elephant in a bed of quicksand. I wore dark glasses during my brief and ever more infrequent appearances on the tour, explaining to the curious that I had been struck on the eye by a golf ball.

Now my life was a gypsy existence in which I traveled from one rest home to another. In one place alone I spent more than $11,000, in addition to constant "tips" to the nurses so that they would give me immediate attention when I wanted it. I went to Saul Clinic in Philadelphia, visited a psychiatrist in Atlanta, twice became so violent that on both occasions I was put in a strait jacket, and another time had the delirium tremens so badly that the only way the doctor on hand could bring me out of them was to inject a half-pint of whiskey into my rectum for a more rapid effect.

In a desperate, last-ditch effort to save my business on the tour, I put my nephew Candler Spence on the job. But the sponsors demanded my presence so I chucked the whole business. What to do? At the time I owned a large building in which I had an office and two

126   GOLF PRO FOR GOD

apartments in Columbia, real estate in Dunedin, Florida, two trailers worth $12,000, and three automobiles.

Enlarging my office at home, I opened a business to distribute golf items in the tri-state area of Georgia and the Carolinas, as well as a shop to reshaft and refinish clubs. I was still able to make out handsomely when I worked, but I worked less and less, and no business can survive under such conditions. So now I started to run out of money.

First I sold a car, then one of the trailers, and then the property in Florida. I'd buy a pint of whiskey and spill it all over me so that any rest home on my long list would let me in and give me drugs to get me "off the whiskey." Now I couldn't afford special nurses any more and it was strictly cash on the barrelhead if I wanted a "treatment."

The last tournament I worked for myself was the Masters in 1957, and then only because my long-time friend Ed Dudley took pity on me. Ed liked to drink himself and he'd give me enough money for all the whiskey I wanted. But he wouldn't have any part of the dope kick. As the days of the tournament passed I was getting closer and closer to the ragged edge.

"Ed," I told him one night, "let me have a hundred dollars. I have to take Dottie some money."

He handed it over and I drove seventy-five miles to the rest home for a "fix."

I had my remaining trailer at the Masters, one which had cost me $7,000. The next day back at the course I ran into a fellow who operated a driving range.

"I need cash fast," I told him. "Will you loan me a couple of hundred dollars?"

"How about selling me that trailer?" he asked.

I couldn't quibble. I needed money for more dope. "Okay, I'll let you have it for $3,000."

I think he had heard somewhere about my "illness." He grinned at me and said, "I'll give you a thousand bucks."

"You crazy, man?" I asked indignantly, spinning on my heel and starting to walk away. I took about ten steps and realized that a thousand dollars would put me back into the good graces of the rest home. So I turned around and went back to where he was still standing.

"Okay. I'll take the thousand."

He shook his head. "The offer is down to $750 and dropping fast," he laughed.

Every foul word in the world bubbled at my lips but I grated my teeth and stuck out my hand. "Okay, friend, you win. Let me have the $750."

That money kept me in the rest home five days, after which I called Dottie to come and pick me up. For some reason or other she was delayed, and the longer I waited the more nervous I became. When she did arrive I was in a vicious mood because I was in a hurry to get home to where I had stashed away a bottle of paraldehyde against a day of dire necessity. This was the day. When we arrived home I rushed into the house, gave myself a giant jolt, and went to sleep.

During the night I was awakened by Dottie's moans.

I didn't know it, but she was having a severe gall-bladder attack. My only thought was to have another shot of paraldehyde but I couldn't find the bottle. Mother and my brother Bob were there with Dottie, and I began swearing and raging through the house, upsetting furniture, smashing dishes, and looking in cupboards, all the while accusing them of hiding my "medicine."

Bob tried to quiet me and I knocked him down the stairs. "Get up and find my bottle," I screamed at Dottie, who was lying there in excruciating pain waiting for an ambulance my mother had called. "You're all trying to kill me. Well, I'll kill all of you first."

I ran to a closet in my room and, with fumbling fingers, loaded a twenty-gauge over-and-under shotgun, the same one I had carried for so long when I was trying to find and kill Harry Miller.

"Find that bottle," I screamed, "or everybody in the house gets it!"

My mother was standing at the bottom of the stairs and I started weaving my way down while aiming the shotgun at her. She opened the door and ran outside. I followed her, prowling like a jungle cat through the yard and out into a nearby field, but I couldn't find her. Well, Dottie would know where that bottle was, I figured, so I went yelling back into the house and stumbled up the stairs. The ambulance had arrived at about this time and, unknown to me, somebody hearing the disturbance had called the police.

I was standing there holding the shotgun on Dottie and yelling insanely for her to get up and find that bottle of paraldehyde when the police chief rushed into the room, sized up the situation in one glance, and knocked me unconscious with a blow on the back of my neck.

I woke up in the same hospital where they were operating on Dottie. Only I was in a strait jacket.

A public hospital can't handle dope cases as extreme as mine, which is why the private rest homes flourish. They tried to wean me from the habit, but it was a whisper in a maelstrom, for they had neither the means nor the ability to cure me. Nor did anyone understand how very many people were in the same shape as I, in constant, searing pain and never-ending desperation. Dottie's operation was a success and, once free of restraint, I simply got up one afternoon, put on my clothes, and walked out of the hospital.

When I got home, my mother pleaded with me. I couldn't see it at the moment, but she had the right formula if I had but listened.

"Son," she said with tears streaming down her cheeks, "please come back to God."

Curtly I turned my back. "Don't worry," I said, "I'll make it my own way."

I went right out and sold Dottie's car, leaving us with one station wagon, and used the money to buy more drugs. After that was gone—and I have no memory of Christmas that winter of 1957—I mortgaged the building in which I had my showroom and the two apartments. This money, too, went for "medicine."

By May of 1958 I was getting frantic over my dwindling funds, and desperately began trying to find a job without telling anybody that I was an addict. Getting on the phone, I contacted Gary Nixon and asked him if I could run his open-air shop at White Sulphur Springs during the Sam Snead Festival. Gary and I agreed on terms, and I went up there after getting together enough Demerol pills to last me a week.

That Sunday on which the tournament ended, the last time I ever trod a golf course on a Sunday, I handled the microphone on the eighteenth green. I was high on my pills and, with $500 I had earned, in a jolly mood; the old-time life of the party.

But once the ceremonies were over and the sun set, it became extremely cold up there in the mountains; and when a couple of friends came by the shop as I was cleaning up, I sent a boy for two quarts of whiskey. I chased the last of my Demerol tablets with a water glass filled with whiskey. Later we sent for more liquor.

I have no memory of leaving White Sulphur Springs. However, several days later, when I came to my senses, I was back in the rest home, and stone broke. A new group had taken over and bilked me of my money.

"You've been here a week," I was told. "You don't have any money and you'll have to leave."

They threw me out and I stood forlornly in the driveway, unshaven, palsied, and without a dime to my name. Somehow, and again I don't remember how, I made my way to Columbia and looked up a number of "friends" in an effort to borrow money. Nobody would loan me as much as a dollar. On a back street I ran into a long-time friend who also was an alcoholic. He had a pint of whiskey and, sitting in the doorway of a closed store, we drank it down.

Reclining there on the dirty step with rain falling just outside the perimeter of our feet, I looked at myself honestly for the first time in seeming ages. My shoes were muddy, there was a large hole in the knee of one trouser leg where I must have fallen, my hands were grimy, my wrists were knobby pipestems, my shirt was stained from where I had been sick to my stomach, and my face bore a two-day growth of beard. I was a bum. And, I realized, I was at the end of the road. As it says in Isaiah 28:8, "For all tables are full of vomit and filthiness, so that there is no place clean."

Struggling to my feet, I didn't even say goodbye to my friend. I walked off through the rain to ask one last favor, for I had decided that the time had come to destroy myself, and the river wasn't too far away. But first, for some unknown reason, I wanted to see the country club I used to own.

I trudged weakly to the house of a man for whom I had done many favors in the past, all the while barely able to stay on my feet. He stared at me when he came to the door in answer to my knock, and I could see the shocked amazement on his face.

"Look," I told him hurriedly before he might shut me out, my voice a weak whisper, "I don't want anything from you, no money or anything. But will you please give me a ride across the river to my old club?"

There was a moment's silence. Then he nodded. "Wait, I'll get the car."

While we were riding, he broke the silence abruptly. "Johnny, I hear what's been going on. You ought to be in a government hospital. You were in service and they'll take care of you."

It had been more than a week since I had eaten a mouthful of food, my nerves were bleeding raw in my need for drugs so that I shook all over like a dog coming out of water and, on the verge of complete collapse, I was so weak that I couldn't figure where I would get the strength to walk down to the riverbank. But inside of me there still was that false pride.

"No," I replied, feeling a strange surprise that while I tried to speak normally my voice was a barely audible whisper.

"Well then, what are your plans?"

It was a painful effort to turn my head so that I could see the vague outline of his head in the semi-darkness. "Plans? None, except that I'm not coming back across the river."

It shocked him into silence. When we arrived at a spot near my old club, I told him to stop and let me out. But I couldn't move.

"You'll have to open the door for me," I said in that husky whisper. "Help me get out."

He came around the car, opened the door, and reached in his hand. As he pulled me forward, I slid off the seat and fell forward into the mud. Suddenly movement was beyond me. I was, it flashed through my mind, going to die right here. But my friend lifted me up without seeming effort, I was so emaciated, and put me back on the seat of his car.

"Now look, Johnny," he told me. "I'm not going to leave you here lying in the mud and the rain. You can't even stand up. Please, let me take you over to the government hospital."

His voice sounded far away and I knew, in the opaque darkness settling over me, that I had already caused him far too much trouble. From somewhere I gathered enough strength to mumble that it would be all right. Then the skyrockets burst inside my head, and I tumbled end over end into a black pit of nothingness.

It wasn't until much later that I learned he had driven me to the hospital and there I had been admitted as a mental case. Because the next thing I knew was dimly understanding that I was dying in that small barred room in the psychiatric ward with the guard watching me through the peephole; the doctor talking about men such as I who wanted nothing more than to die; the nurse giving vocal thanks that the morgue had been enlarged recently; and the chaplain getting down on his knees and interceding with God for me.

What followed was my own personal miracle, and I can only thank God and pray that somehow my torturous trip through an earthly purgatory will help in some small way to aid others in seeing the saving light. For, as it says in Mark 9:27:

"But Jesus took him by the hand, and lifted him up; and he arose."

Spence and friend, Phil Harris, at the Fort Wayne Open, Ind., 1952. American Motors Corporation.

8

My Lord, if now I have found favor in thy sight, pass not away, I pray thee, from thy servant. *Genesis 18:3*

God Sets Up a Meeting

Every Friday to me is Good Friday. Many people think of it as being only that Friday on which Jesus was crucified. I like to think of it as being a Friday which brought me up and raised me from the dead—because it was Friday, June 20, 1958, when I made a decision that ended years of misery and gave me life eternal.

That was the night when, at Emory Harper's invitation, I accepted Christ in the hospital chapel.

Fourteen weeks later, still weak and frightfully underweight, I caught a ride to Charlotte, North Carolina, a distance of ninety miles from Columbia, because I wanted to hear Billy Graham. I was waiting outside at the back entrance of the Charlotte coliseum and auditorium, merely hoping to get a glimpse of him, when Graham arrived with a large group which included the fellow ministers who are known as his teammates. In the party were Grady Wilson, T. W. Wilson, and a number of others.

I had met Billy Graham about three or four years earlier at the Augusta National Golf Club when I was associated with Ed Dudley, the head professional there at that time. One day—and I'll never forget it, because the young governor of Tennessee, Frank Clements, arrived with Billy—someone came in and said they had arrived at the club. At the time we were in the back of the shop drinking highballs and playing cards.

Looking out the window, I saw them approaching and I joked, "All right, fellows, we have to break it up. Put the cards away and hide the booze because we've got two fanatics coming. When they get out on the course we can start up again, but we'd better try to be nice while they're here."

However, on this particular Friday night in Charlotte, during the Billy Graham Crusade of September and October of 1958, I had been a Christian fourteen weeks to the night. God really set up this meeting, because Billy Graham spotted me, alone in the crowd. Coming over to me, he asked me to go inside with him to his combination office and dressing room. "I'd like to speak to you a few minutes, Johnny," he said.

We went in and sat there chatting for a short while. Then he looked me right in the eye, and his voice was extremely serious.

"Johnny, many people say that when some people are converted it doesn't last. I know that you've only been a convert now for a relatively short time."

I agreed. "Yes, for only fourteen weeks, yet I'll never take another drink or shot of dope. But Billy, I'd like to ask you a question. How did you know about me?"

His face lighted up with a brief smile and then became serious again. "When I was preaching at the Cow Palace at San Francisco in June, word came to me about you. Of course I had known you just briefly, but I knew about you, and also that a number of people were praying for you. I heard, when I was in San Francisco, that you had been saved."

I was amazed, and I told him so. I also mentioned the incident at Augusta and how, while now I felt differently, there still were many customers for his great work.

"Because in this psychiatric ward where they had me, we were allowed to stay up an extra half hour on Saturday night so we could watch television. They all damned you because the channel which carried your program was the only one with good local reception. Most of the patients wanted to watch a western program, but on that channel all they could get were those lines that look like Venetian blinds. Everybody growled disgustedly and wished you were on the station with the poor reception.

"But I felt a lot different about you," I added. "And I'm sorry about when you and Governor Clements came in down at Augusta."

Billy smiled again. "Johnny, tonight I'm preaching on conversion. I'm preaching from the Book of Hebrews, the second chapter, third verse, which says, 'How shall we escape, if we neglect so great salvation.' And Johnny, many people are neglecting that life eternal which God has promised us, just because they haven't been told in a way they'll understand."

He looked steadily at me for a moment. "I wonder if you'd get up here tonight and tell these people? Many people say that it doesn't last. But Emory Harper is here and he's been converted more than eight years, and I'd just like for people to see you and hear . . ."

I burst in and cut him off. "Oh, no sir, Mr. Graham, I couldn't do that. I couldn't possibly do it. I wouldn't have the slightest idea what to say."

"Just tell them what's in your heart."

I was so apprehensive I could hardly talk. But I finally stuttered another refusal. "Well, Mr. Graham, I just wouldn't know what to say. I've never really studied the Bible. I'm not a minister and I just can't see me getting up there in front of all those people."

"It certainly would mean a lot to me, and to everybody else," he cut in, "to hear you say with your own lips, to confess, that you really believe what's in your own heart. That God raised Jesus from the dead and that you believe it."

His voice became stern and he pointed a finger at me. "Are you ashamed?"

I thought a minute. Then I told him, "Mr. Graham, I made a promise to God not long ago that I'd never be ashamed of my love for him. I don't have the slightest idea what I'd say, but I guess even the little I know of the Bible covers that for me."

He nodded then and, as if testing me, asked, "In what place, Johnny?"

"In Matthew, the nineteenth and twentieth verses of the tenth chapter," I said, quoting from memory:

"But when they deliver you up, take no thought how or what ye shall speak: for it shall be given you in that same hour what ye shall speak.

"For it is not ye that speak, but the Spirit of your Father which speaketh in you."

A smile lit up his face. "Praise the Lord, Johnny. Let's pray."

We both got down on our knees beside a couch in his dressing room. I didn't pray but I listened to him pray. I've heard him pray many times since, and been with him quite a bit, but I've never heard him pray more diligently. I've never heard him more fervent in seeking the Lord's ear than he was that night in his effort to give me strength and the ability to stand up and speak.

When he closed his prayer, we went upstairs together. Then, because of the tremendous crowd and because his entrance was listed for a certain time, he asked Grady Wilson and T. W. Wilson to take me the rest of the way to the dais. There I met Cliff Barrows, Billy's announcer and director of music, as well as George Beverly Shea, the team's soloist.

They made we welcome with smiles, warm words, and firm handclasps, and I was given a seat in what I suppose, if you weren't a Christian, you'd refer to as the VIP section, because I guess only the important preachers—the Very Important Preachers—were supposed to be there.

Out in front of me it seemed as if there was an ocean of faces, for the coliseum was filled to overflowing. I felt a chill come over me. How in the world, I asked myself, can you get up and talk in front of all these people, Johnny Spence? What I wanted was out, and fast.

I started to get up and run for it, but Grady Wilson, one of Billy's dearest friends and the one who reads the Scripture for him on every program, reached over and put a restraining hand on my shoulder.

"Johnny, where are you going?"

"I thought I'd walk outside, Reverend Wilson. Just sort of walk around a little bit."

"Well, why are you going?"

"I'm cold. I thought I'd just warm up a little."

He smiled at me. "That's odd. Look out there at all those thousands of people, Johnny. They're fanning themselves. They're not cold."

He had me there. So I took another tack. "Well, Dr. Wilson, I've got low blood pressure."

Still smiling, he pushed down on my shoulder. "Sit still a minute, Johnny, I want to talk to you."

"This low blood pressure's rough," I countered desperately.

"I know all about it. I've got it, too. Let's sit down and talk about it. Actually, Johnny, you know that if you get up and leave, we'll never see you again, partner. What you are feeling is the Devil speaking to you. He wants to get you out of here because he doesn't think you're in the right place."

So I sat back with a helpless feeling, and Grady Wilson asked, "Johnny, do you know how many people are out here in this coliseum?"

"I ought to," I groaned. "I've counted every one of them."

He laughed. "We'll have 13,500 in here and 2,500 next door in the auditorium on closed-circuit television. There also will be many thousands listening in on radio."

This information didn't help me at all, for now I really started shaking in earnest. But Grady Wilson reached over and placed his hand on my Bible, which Mother had given me on June 26, six days after I accepted Jesus Christ as my Lord and Saviour. His voice was so low that only I could hear him.

"Johnny, 'seek ye first the kingdom of God, and his righteousness,' as we are told in Matthew 6:33. Do that, and all these things that you think about shall be added unto you. So let's sit here and pray."

I wasn't used to praying, particularly in front of so many people. But Grady Wilson sat there and prayed for me, in a low voice which reached only my ears. Slowly my anxiety seemed to fade away.

Shortly afterward, Billy Graham came in and sat down near me. He glanced over at me with a firm, determined look, his chin jutting out. Bunching one fist, he shook it at me quickly in a gesture of comradeship and confidence which could only be interpreted as meaning "Get in there and fight 'em, boy."

When it came time, and he introduced me, he brought a roar from the crowd by saying, "I want to introduce one of my grandchildren tonight. He's a golf professional from down in South Carolina. The last time he was here, he was with Miss America, Lee Ann Merriwether. Tonight he has come in under a different banner. Tonight I want to introduce him as my grand-child."

When I arose at his beckoning and walked what seemed to be ten miles to that elevated pulpit, there was a real roar because everyone could see that I was old enough to be his big brother, if not his father. But he explained his meaning to them.

"Johnny is a product of God's word as we are told in Isaiah, the fifty-fifth chapter and the eleventh verse: 'So shall my word be that goeth forth out of my mouth: it shall not return unto me void, but it shall accomplish that which I please, and it shall prosper in the thing whereto I sent it.'"

He told them, too, how God's word had come to Emory Harper in 1950 through him, and that it was Harper in turn who saved me.

"So I feel tonight that when Johnny Spence stands before you, he is one of my spiritual grandchildren," Billy told the audience. "And now, Johnny, tell them what is in your heart."

It was as if those last few steps to the pulpit required an eternity. But suddenly there I was, and, as the Bible promised, the words came forth.

"Ladies and Gentlemen, I don't know enough about the Bible. I've only been converted a few weeks. But I do know the first verse I read after I raised my hand and publicly, unashamedly, said yes, that through faith I would take this step toward God.

"This verse was held up in front of me by a chaplain and again by Mr. Harper at my request. What little bit I could read, they had to focus for me, as if they were sliding a trombone in and out, for I only had vision in one eye; the other had been torn out, and the sight was gone. But I shall always remember every word of this verse because every word means something to me: II Corinthians 5·17

" 'Therefore, if any man be in Christ, he is a new creature: old things are passed away; behold, all things are become new.'

"And, ladies and gentlemen, I'll tell you, when I read that verse—and I have read it over and over again countless times—God was speaking to me, saying that if any one is in Christ, he is a Christian. If any one is in Christ, these old things that he did, he possibly may do again, but he won't want to do them. Because he still may have a carnal mind in a carnal body, and he'll be here with this sinful world. But God has promised he will give me protection and that I will be in the world but not of the world. I have taken that into my heart, and I will claim his promises, that he will never leave me nor forsake me."

Strangely, I thought as I spoke, I wasn't the least bit nervous. And I went on, as if I had been speaking from the pulpit all my life, to tell them that I had read in Hebrews about the protection God offers, and that we can claim these promises. He tells us in Hebrews 13:5, 'I will never leave thee, nor forsake thee.' When God

says there is only black or white, he must either be
telling the truth or telling a lie. I wouldn't call my God,
my Father, a liar, because if you do you disbelieve,
and that is when you have to go to hell. When people
blaspheme the Holy Spirit, it is only because they disbelieve in God, our Father and Creator.

"I'm going to believe without question," I told them.
"I know I'll get kicked. I know it won't be easy. But
I'm going to believe and claim those promises every
time I feel low and sad. I'm going to leave the rest up
to God because I know full well what hell is. I've tasted
of hell and I want no more of it, so that anything at all
he can offer me has to be better than what I've had."

It had been pouring out so rapidly I had to pause for
breath. Then I told them, "Thank you for letting me
come up here tonight. Not as a preacher, not as a golf
professional, but as a man who was dead in his sins,
and who now is alive because God loved me so much
and did so much for me."

When I sat down, Dr. Graham preached a sermon
on conversion from Hebrews 2:3: "How shall we escape, if we neglect so great salvation; which at the first
began to be spoken by the Lord, and was confirmed
unto us by them that heard him."

I learned a great deal that night, for Dr. Graham
spoke of the gift that God had presented to us, this son
of his who died for our sins, and that he had paid the
ransom. He pointed out that it didn't cost us a nickel,
but that it was freely given to those who would have
faith, and all we had to do was to take that one step to
merit salvation.

When the meeting was over, Billy extended his invitation for conversion and several hundred people responded. They came forward because they had listened to God's word: they had been instructed that this was the time, and that God only speaks to us one time. I gave thanks that I had learned this, as well as for the fact that it is such a wonderfully simple act for those who will open their hearts and listen.

After this ended, Billy requested me to go into the counseling room where others waited. Once more I was asked to speak a few words. I didn't really know what to say. So I told them, "Folks, I want you to pray for me. I'm the biggest sinner that ever got up here, and I know I'm worse than anybody who ever came in here. So I want you to pray for me."

A few minutes later I was approached by the members of Dr. Graham's team. They asked me to go with them and appear on television so that I could be interviewed by Grady Wilson, Billy's associate evangelist, and Cliff Barrows, the music director. We went there for a half-hour program.

I was asked about drugs, about alcohol, and what I thought was the cure. All I could answer was the truth as I saw it through my newly opened one eye.

"God spoke to me," I said. "If a man had robbed a bank, he was a robber. If a man had committed a murder, he was a murderer. If a man had committed rape, he was known as a rapist. If a man had become an alcoholic, it was because of alcohol.

"It seems to me," I added, "that God has spoken to us all, that these are sinful acts, first breaking God's

Commandments and then man's laws. If you move it all under S-I-N, you've got it covered because Christ died for your sins."

Later I found it almost beyond comprehension when I received hundreds of letters seeking counsel. Asking counsel from me—a man who had only been saved a few weeks himself!

Fortunately for me, and I say this with all credit to Billy Graham and his whole team, those dedicated men gave me added help by telling me when I left that night to go back home with the supporting strength of their brotherhood.

"Johnny, read that word, study it, and be careful and guard it zealously, because many people are going to try to break you down and tear you up with it. Remember, the Bible says 'neither cast ye your pearls before swine, lest they trample them under their feet, and turn again and rend you.' These things God tells us may happen to forewarn us. So keep the faith."

It was a memorable night, one I shall never forget. And since then I have been a fast friend of Dr. Graham and his team. We have played golf together, which they all enjoy, and we are brothers in the Lord. The Bible says in I Corinthians that we know we've passed from eternal death and damnation into eternal life because of one thing, because we love our brethren.

To me all of this has opened up a brand-new, clean and shining, wonderful world. My heart swells with rejoicing when I read Revelation 21:1:

"And I saw a new heaven and a new earth: for the first heaven and the first earth were passed away . . ."

Neva Jane Langley, Miss America, 1953, a guest at the University of Michigan's golf course in the International J.C. golf championship. Spence is at the microphone.

9

There was a man of the Pharisees, named Nicodemus, a ruler of the Jews: The same came to Jesus by night . . . *John 3:1–2*

Just Working for the Lord

I felt, during the days after I left the hospital where I had been saved, and while I slowly regained my strength, that I owed a great debt of gratitude and thanksgiving. For weeks I pondered how I could make a contribution which would help others, and then the Lord showed me the way.

The tiny building which the hospital called a chapel, and where I had reached Jesus Christ through the help of Emory Harper, was a ramshackle affair, small and inadequate. Even though I was penniless, I decided that in my infinite gratitude I would build a new chapel at the hospital, which would be open to those of all religious denominations.

My first step was to consult an architect, and he co-operated by drawing up the plans for the building I contemplated. "But it will cost at least $220,000," he frowned. "Johnny, where in the world will you be able to raise that kind of money?"

Where indeed? But I smiled because of an inner confidence I couldn't explain, and told him, "The Lord will provide."

How to start? I pondered. Golf was all I knew, actually. Well, then, I told myself, you'd better start with golf. If through golf I could earn money for my own selfish purposes, surely I could do the same for God.

Ultimately I decided that I would open my chapel fund drive with a golf exhibition between two top players. Then, if I could get the necessary cooperation for my project, I would film it in color and show it before various church groups and allied organizations who, for its use, might make contributions toward the building fund.

To get the project off the ground, first of all I had to have the players. So I went to Sam Snead and Mike Souchak, two of the finest players in the world, and men who are particularly well loved and admired throughout the South. Both of them agreed without hesitation to play the exhibition for nothing when I explained to them about my proposed project.

Through Billy Graham I also managed to obtain the assistance of a motion-picture company which filmed the match for me without any cost.

The exhibition was played in the spring of 1961, tee-
ing off my chapel fund drive, and the response both
during the match and afterward, with the showing of
the film, exceeded my fondest hopes. The money eventually was raised, and the chapel at long last was con-
structed.

Shortly after it was finished, I went to the Masters
to watch some of the early practice rounds and happened to see Snead, long a favorite of mine, putting on
the practice green. I didn't approach him but stood off
by myself, outside the ropes, watching him. Finally, he
happened to look up and spot me. In a few minutes he
beckoned to me, and I stepped over the ropes and went
to him.

"Johnny," he said, stroking a putt smoothly, "what
ever happened to that chapel you were going to build?"

"It's all built, Sam," I told him, "thanks to you and
Mike and a lot of other wonderfully generous people."

"It's built?" he repeated, astonishment written on his
face. "You mean to say that through that exhibition you
were able to raise all that money?"

"That's right, Sam, and I'll never be able to thank
you enough for your help. But the Lord knows what you
did, you and Mike."

Sam stood there shaking his head as if unable to believe what I had told him.

Snead always was a man who took excellent care of
himself physically, which is one of the reasons why he
still was able to win tournaments even when he was in
his fifties. His fellow professionals always prodded Sam
about being ultracautious with a dollar, and, I believe
sincerely, Sam nurtured this image because early in his

career he was taken a number of times for a soft touch.

Now, as we stood on the putting green at the Augusta National Golf Club, where I once had been one of the gayest blades but now was a virtually ignored unknown, Sam looked around to see that no one was within hearing distance. Then, in a low voice, he said, "You see, Johnny, old Sam ain't so bad."

"Of course you're not, Sam," I agreed. "Without your help I'm sure the chapel would never have been finished."

Sam again scanned the area to make certain that no one could overhear us. "You know, Johnny, they were trying to raise money for a new organ at our church up in West Virginia. Well, they were a couple of hundred dollars short, so I donated the money."

"Sam, that's really wonderful," I said. "Did you get right up in church and make the donation?"

Snead frowned at me and looked about nervously. "Not on your life, John. You think I wanted all those folks to see Sam giving away all that money? No, sir. I went over to the preacher's house at night, knocked on the door, and when he came I just pushed the money into his hands and took off."

I had to chuckle at the mental picture Sam had painted. "You remind me," I laughed, "of Nicodemus."

Sam had bent down over his putter, but that remark brought him upright with a puzzled look on his face. "Nicky? Nicky who?" he asked with a frown.

"Nicodemus."

Sam rubbed his nose and squinted in deep thought. "Nicky Demus? John, where at is he the pro?"

I do not tell this story to ridicule Sam, who quietly does many generous acts. But I wanted to drive home to him that Nicodemus, too, went to Jesus by night lest it be known that he was on the Lord's work.

"You should have stood right up in church on Sunday and made your contribution," I advised Sam, "because it says in John 3:21: 'But he that doeth truth cometh to the light, that his deeds may be made manifest, that they are wrought in God.'"

I am not too certain that I made my point. For there is a bewildering reluctance on the part of most athletes to let it be known that they are good Christians, let alone to have it made public that they work for God. Many of them undoubtedly have the feeling that they might not be regarded as "he-men," while still others to whom I have talked consider those who make a public display of their faith as "some kind of a nut."

There is no doubt in my mind but that many people classify me in this latter category, but it bothers me not one whit. I never preach, sermonize, or advance my religious thoughts to others unless they ask me to do so. If I am asked, I am only too glad to try in my own small way to help.

Certainly there is nothing sissified or "nutty" about athletes with whom I work in trying to help others—men such as Bobby Richardson, a long-time star second baseman for the New York Yankees; Jerry Kendall, second baseman for the Minnesota Twins; or Ray Berry, an end for the Baltimore Colts of the National Professional Football League. They are great athletes, but they are also decent and intelligent young men who are dedicated to working for God. They are not ashamed of their Christian efforts, and find no need to cover their labors by night in the manner of Nicodemus.

When, after having been cleansed, I first began to get back my strength, I had no idea what I might be able to do. I thought I was positively through with golf, among other things feeling that the temptations of the old days might be too great.

Billy Graham changed this defensive type of thinking for me, convincing me first, once and for all, that as long as I looked to God I could resist any temptations.

"I am certain of that," he told me, "and, Johnny, you must take into consideration that this is the field in which you can do the most good. There isn't another man in golf who will take a stand for God through Christ. I have prayed that you will remain in golf, in some fashion or other, because it will give you entree into places where preachers and evangelists cannot go."

I accepted his decision and, while only the Lord knows if I have done any good in helping others as a direct result of accepting Graham's advice, I give praise to God for reuniting me with my father before he died.

As I related earlier, my father had separated from my mother and had left home when I was just barely fourteen years old. Although I had seen him on occasion, and actually at one stage worked for a company which he headed, we had not visited with each other since the day he left us.

A couple of years ago I was offered a site about fifteen miles from Columbia where I might be able to set up a driving range and teach golf. As I say, if you don't want to work at a golf course on Sunday—something which I will never do—it is practically impossible to get a job in this sport which I love so much. No matter in which direction I turned, I was rejected and often scorned because of this stand I had taken for Christianity.

It wasn't that I was militantly opposing them so much as the fact that I wouldn't join them in their destruction of the Sabbath.

Once I had owned a golf club in Columbia, but now I no longer was welcome at any of the major courses. As an example, in trying to earn money while fighting my way back to health, I even resorted to teaching at a local driving range at a small par three course, but I finally was told in no uncertain terms not to come there any more. The other country clubs in the area made it brutally obvious that I was persona non grata.

A group of men in Lexington County, about fifteen miles away, had told me that if I came over there they would let me use their property for this driving range if it was a satisfactory site. By this time, I had been let down many times by people who said they wanted to help me but who really were only concerned with making money off their own property at my expense and effort.

As I drove out toward this new site, not really believing that my trip would come to anything, I came to a side road which led up to a large farm which I knew that my father owned.

I had no plan to go see my father but God led me up that road.

I'd heard my father had been sick and, not even knowing whether he was home, I drove up the road to the farmhouse, pulled into the yard, and saw him sitting on the porch in a rocking chair, with a shawl around his shoulders. Carrying my Bible, I walked up onto the porch and, shaking hands with him, said, "Hello, Pop. I thought it was about time I came to see you."

"I'm glad to see you," he greeted me. "What are you doing over this way?"

"Well, just going over to see some fellows. I thought I'd stop over and see how you were doing."

"I'm glad to have you," he said, pulling the shawl tighter around his shoulders.

As I sat there, I thought of how much I loved this man, and how heartbroken I had been when he left home. I remembered how many times I had been drunk and sick and how, during those terrible days, I had felt a terrible hatred for him for what I thought he had done to me.

We talked awhile, about the weather and people we knew, and as I prepared to leave he looked up at me and asked, "Son, do you need any money?"

"No, sir."

"Well, what are you doing?"

"Pop," I told him, "I'm just working for the Lord."

"I don't quite understand," he said, rocking a little faster.

"It's this way," I explained. "I have had the blessing of support and advice from Billy Graham. I go wherever I am invited, tell the people about my miserable life, and explain how I found salvation through Jesus

Christ, in the hope that I will in some fashion be able
to help some other poor souls."

In my Bible I had a little card which I was using as a
bookmark. It was a card with a small message which I
had used on a speaking tour in Pennsylvania where I
had spoken before men's clubs and even at jails and a
penitentiary. I took the card out of the Bible.

"Here, for instance," I said, "is a card: 'Christian
Business Men of Reading, Pennsylvania. Annual Ladies'
Night.' "

Fishing out his spectacles, he held up the card, and
with raised eyebrows observed, "This says two dollars
and fifty cents per person. How many did you have
there?"

"Pop," I told him, "there must have been five hundred people there."

"Did you get this money?"

"No, sir, I didn't."

"Well, what did you get?"

I hesitated only momentarily. Then I told him, "I go
on faith. These men gave me an honorarium, and they
took care of my room and board."

"Looks to me like you ought to get more than that,"
Father said.

"Pop," I told him, "I depend on God. I just depend
on him. He tells me that he will take care of me. He
created the birds and the bees, and us, too; and if I
need anything, he says, he'll take care of me."

I opened my Bible and, asking him to listen, read
him the sixth chapter of Matthew. His rocking chair
creaked back and forth but gradually slowed and was

completely still as I finished the final verse: " 'Take therefore no thought for the morrow: for the morrow shall take thought for the things of itself. Sufficient unto the day is the evil thereof.' "

Looking up, I found him hunched forward motionless in his chair, staring hard at me. He began to rock without comment for a few moments, then stopped again and asked me with intense interest, "Son, do you stick by that Bible pretty close?"

"Pop, I live by it. I have to live by it. It's the only thing I have. I live by God now because I know he loves me."

We fell silent and I got up and told him I had to leave. "Do you mind," I asked, "if I have a word of prayer?"

"Go ahead," he nodded. "Go right ahead."

I got down on my knees by my father's rocker, and I prayed to God from the depths of my grateful heart.

"Father in heaven, I want to thank you for letting me come see my father. I don't know about how Pop feels in his heart but I want him to know, God, that you created both of us. When he left home, he broke my heart, but I love him as much today as I ever did. And if he feels in his heart like I feel, Father in Heaven, then I'm going to see him in the resurrected body you've promised to all of us who believe. You promise this, and it must be true or you wouldn't have told us. God, if he feels the same way about you as I do, this isn't a sad occasion. This is a happy occasion, for we'll be together forever and ever. Thank you, God."

As I arose, my father, a man I'd never seen shed a

tear in his life, was crying. The tears were rolling down his face, and I reached over and kissed him on his cheek.

"Son," he said gruffly, "I want to tell you something. I feel the same way you do about God."

It didn't dawn on me at that moment what he had just done. I was never to see him conscious again. Because four weeks later I was called home from another town with the news that my father had suffered a stroke and had been taken to the Baptist Hospital in Columbia. I raced home and, stopping to pick up Dottie, went on to the hospital. Some members of our family and a minister were there already, and they told me Father had very little chance of living.

We prayed right there in the lobby of the Baptist Hospital. Yet even as I began to tell God how much we wanted my father saved, I thought with a great peace: God, if you take him this second, I know he'll go to heaven.

I was positive of it because, on his porch the day I had stopped to visit him, he had made a simple statement with his lips—that he felt the same way I did about God. I knew that, feeling this way, he was certain of going to heaven.

It is that simple. You have to confess with your mouth and believe with your heart.

"Father, thank you," I prayed, "because I know I'll see my father in heaven."

A few minutes later they told me he had been taken to the recovery room after a six-hour operation to remove a blood clot. I went upstairs and saw him lying

there, pale, unconscious, and breathing with great difficulty, and the nurse told me he didn't have a chance.
He never recovered consciousness.

At the funeral, the minister did not eulogize my
father. He spoke, instead, in praise of God, and of the
eternal decision my father had made just prior to his
last few weeks on earth.

Typical, too, of the fulfillment which comes when
you walk with God was the manner in which my wife
Dottie embraced God.

No woman ever suffered for and from mortal man
more than my wife. Yet, while Mother was always extremely devout, and even after I had been saved, Dottie
was no more than a passive Christian. You may wonder
that my sudden reversal did not convince her.

But I have to give the credit to Henderson Belk, a
dear and wonderful friend. For, right in our kitchen,
he sat across from Dottie and made her see the light.
Possibly you have heard of the Belk family, for they
operate a large chain of stores throughout the South.

They are, I am thankful to say, among those business-
men in the minority who put God ahead of the dollar.

I have been asked many times since I became a living Christian to explain the golfing doctrine that I
teach nowadays. I merely tie in the principle of teaching golf with the principle that is the plan of salvation for everyone that believeth.

God has said throughout the Bible that he is not
willing that any should perish, but that all should be
saved. So he has set down in a principle everything
that we should do or that should be done to glorify him.

The principle I want to explain now is based entirely on God's principle of motivation, centrifugal motion. When I was a young fellow, we used to play a game called pop-the-whip. All that the man standing in the middle had to do was hold hands with the person on each side of him and pivot around. The more people you had in this line, the longer the leverage. The man on the end, if he was far enough out and if he was flung loose, could really be sent sprawling. In a way this proves God's principle of motivation, that a small movement from the center going outward will build speed.

You don't apply speed. You build it. That is the principle. The earth upon which we are standing today turns around. Why does it turn? Well, God knows why it turns, but the principle involved is that of centrifugal motion from the center. If this varied, or were altered, to any degree that a machine could ever figure out, alteration of this principle would fling all of us into space.

So the principle that God has set down can never vary. The Bible tells us, as in the Book of Hebrews, the thirteenth chapter, that God is the same yesterday, today, and tomorrow. His principles through Christ are the same yesterday, today, and tomorrow. So then, as a golf professional, if I teach these principles that God has laid down, we can take a piece of string and tie a small weight on the end of it and begin a whirling motion of this weighted string with our hand. With a small turn of the hand, the barest movement of the hand, the string attached to this little weight creates a circle.

Now, if you don't believe that this principle is powerful, stick your hand into the path of that tiny whirling weight tied to the end of the string. Why? Because the principle involved has built up enough speed to make this a dangerous weapon. Believe it, for with this same principle the tiny David slew the towering Goliath.

This is the principle, once it is harnessed, which can be used for good. We take this principle and we lift up a golf club. The golf club has been dead, an inanimate thing, lying there by itself without a motivating force. I think of Johnny Spence, a golf professional, who was dead in his sins, living the deadly way in which the world wastes its life in conformity. And when Christ lifted me up, as Psalm 40 tells me: ". . . he inclined unto me, and heard my cry.

"He brought me up also out of an horrible pit, out of the miry clay, and set my feet upon a rock, and established my goings."

He brought me alive. And then Christ tells me throughout the four Gospels many things. People say, well, how do you know this? I know because whereas I was blind, now I can see, even as the blind man from whose eyes Jesus pulled the scales. And I tell you that when I teach golf today I use this simple principle of guidance.

Number one is to make a dead thing come alive, as a dead human walking around, born only once and not twice, becomes born twice because God says in the third chapter, seventh verse of the Book of John, "Marvel not that I said unto thee, Ye must be born again." He says you must be born again to see the Kingdom of Heaven. You can't go back into your mother's womb, but this is a rebirth of the spirit. So this is the reason I believe in this principle so much: because it's God's principle. If we can take a dead thing such as a golf club and put it in our hands and with this principle of God's, that of centrifugal motion, we can propel our hands in such a manner that anything from a string and a small heavy object, or a grip and a shaft and a clubhead, can be used in the same identical manner, we can create so much velocity in that clubhead that it strikes a golf ball and propels it forth at a tremendous rate of speed.

This is God's principle at work, so let's use it.

We take the golf club and we put it in our hands. Now we say we want to use this golf club to hit a ball. But no, let's not hit a ball yet. Let's prove this principle of God's, and then we can hit a ball.

You say, well, now, how does this work? How about the great Sam Snead, Arnold Palmer, and Ben Hogan? Do they do this? I don't care who they are. Each one of them uses this principle because he was made by God and he is using God's principle regardless of who gets the credit.

That is what happens with a golf club. We make it alive, even as I became alive in Christ because I reached out. I cried, and Psalms 24, 34, 36, and 37 tell about the poor man who reached out and cried and God took hold of him.

So the next step after the grip is putting your feet in position. Now you have the club in your hands and putting your feet together in position, you can stand right there and use one thought and create the whole circle. Every circle must have a center. As the center of our swing we use the chin. Why not the head, you ask, because it's my head which must remain still? Well, when I say the head, I'm making it complicated: ears, eyes, nose, forehead and hair. But when we say the chin, we pinpoint it. You say, "Well, how about the pronation or the cocking of the wrists?"

Did you know that God put each of us together in a similar manner? Our carpal muscles are all identical. So why then should I tell you to pronate, when you take this club up in your hands with your feet together, put it right in front of your chin and say, "All right, I'm going to swing my hands in a full circle." If you break this down in slow motion, you'll see that the left hand is on top at the back and the right hand is on top at the finish.

But you've only had one thought through the whole thing. Why, then, should I tell you to turn your hands over, when it's going to take place normally and naturally if you have but one thought.

This thought is, and God tells us in the Book of Psalms, that the earth is the Lord's and the fullness thereof. We can think of this, that the principle is God's, so let's think of the fullness of our hands in motion. If I think of my hands making a circle, they automatically go back with the golf club, so I don't have to think of taking them back. If I think of my hands making a full circle, I don't have to think of them going through. But if I stop to analyze each move, then my mind cannot work as fast as my hands. The hand is quicker even than the eye, so what will we do? We stop and we pronate. We move to this position and then to that position.

I talked to one famous golfer who told me that he had written no less than five whole books on how to play golf. So it doesn't take too much perception to see how much confusion is being created. I have nothing against this man. But he admitted the more he wrote, the more he was paid. So this comes back to profit again.

Now then, let us once more go into fullness. We take the hands and make a circle, and we go through with it completely. You can check this out because God is the truth. Jesus Christ says, "I am the way," and in 14:6, in the Book of John, it reads: ". . . I am the way, the truth, and the life."

Jesus says let's tell the truth.

If you'll check this out in slow motion, with the hands up in front of the chin, holding the chin still, you can just think of making a big circle with your hands and the fullness thereof. Slow motion will show you the left hand is on top at the backswing and the right hand is on top when you finish the full swing. And, at the moment of impact, you are in perfect position and you only had one thought in mind.

This is the amazing thing about doing it God's way. When we take this thing in sequence, one, two, three, and go through with it, then we have created a perfect circle. You may say to me, "That sounds pretty good, but then what do you do about it?"

I say, "Then you have faith." Did you know that blind

faith is the thing that we must have—faith without fear? God tells us this in the eleventh chapter of Hebrews: "Without faith it is impossible to please Him." So what you need is faith in God's way to do it.

If you'll check this out in slow motion, with the

One of my greatest pleasures was to teach Bobby Richardson to play golf. You have probably heard of Bobby; he is the star second baseman for the New York Yankees. Bobby comes from Sumter, South Carolina, a neighbor town to my own home town of Columbia. Bobby came well equipped to learn—besides being a great athlete, he is a dedicated Christian whose purpose in life is to please God every day of his life. He realizes that it is God who has given him the ability, the opportunity and certainly any earthly glory that comes from being a famous baseball player. Bobby enjoys playing ball because he feels that is where God would have him serve.

I took him to a golf course in Sumter. No sooner had I produced the clubs than Bobby said, "Just give me those clubs and I'll take it from there. We probably won't win the United States Open but we ought to have some fun." I think that comment of Bobby's is a demonstration of the power of blind faith. Bobby trusts, as he gives thanks, in his God-given abilities, abilities that enable a man to overcome even seemingly insuperable obstacles, both in the playing field and in life itself.

"Bobby," I told him, "playing golf for fun isn't half as difficult as most people think. Actually, I can teach you everything I know about golf in ten minutes."

Richardson, a small, thin man, looked puzzled. "Johnny, from what I've been told in the past and what I have read about this game, it requires more than ten minutes to take just one golf lesson."

"Shucks, Bobby," I said, "one time I wrote a series of articles on golf instruction for the newspapers, and it took me six weeks to get the club down from the top of the backswing to the ball. But stretching it out like that isn't only a lot of nonsense; it isn't Christian."

I explained to him my principle of motivation, that theory of centrifugal motion producing speed through God's doing, and how we make the club come alive with our hands.

"Bobby, it's a simple matter of one, two, three, four. Any man who can count to four can swing a golf club. Now understand, I don't say he'll play championship golf, because that takes a lot of practice to develop touch and feel and to put that little old ball into the cup. But I do say that anyone can swing the club well.

"So what do we do mechanically? Well, Bobby, we hold the club properly in our hands, hold it evenly with all ten fingers, and work the hands as a unit. You have that, okay, so forget the hands. Now you put the clubhead behind the ball with your feet together. This is step number two, putting our feet together so that we can start from the center, because all good things come from the center of life, which is Jesus Christ, and with our eyes on him we cannot go wrong. So we start from the center."

Bobby listened attentively and followed my directions without comment. So I continued.

"Now a lot of people ask me how far out do I put my left foot, and what about the right foot. I can't tell them that. I couldn't tell a man from the size of his foot that he should move it just so far when he walks, so I don't tell him how to place his feet when he gets up to a golf ball. I just tell him which one to move first. God does the rest."

This had him thinking, I could see, and I went right ahead.

"Look at it this way: if you put the club behind the ball and the hands are kept still, and you move your left foot out first if you are right-handed and your right foot out first if you are left-handed, the front foot will always drop into position automatically in relation to the club you are using and the length of the shaft of that particular club. Then you move the back foot out from the center and it, too, will automatically drop into the proper position.

"Now we have taken the first step by positioning the hands, and the second step by positioning the feet, and you forget them. Why? Because God doesn't want us to be slothful, so why should you get a good grip and a good stance and go back over them? That's one, two, one, and we should keep things in order. What we want is one, two, three, four.

"So we take step number three, which is positioning the chin. You will hear it said many times that you should keep your head steady. That takes in the eyes, ears, nose, and even your eyebrows. But we point the chin to stabilize the head because every true circle must have a center, and you'll have one if you lock that chin in position. So, with one, two, and three accomplished, all we have to do in step number four is swing that club in a good, full circle. That's all there is to it. Sure, you can read many confusing things, such as pronation and what have you. But hold that club out in front of you on a horizontal plane. Swing it back like a baseball bat and the left hand has to be on top. Swing on through and your right hand has to wind up on top. Do it from behind a golf ball and, with a good full circle, the same thing has to happen.

"That, Pardner," I finished, "is the only golf lesson, in essence, that anyone could give you, and it's God's own lesson."

After that we played, and Bobby told me he hit the ball better than he ever had when he was younger. He enjoyed it, too. I know because he told me so.

Yet I know without the slightest shadow of a doubt that my system does work. All it requires is blind faith, and I have solid proof.

I spoke at the Veterans Hospital in Columbia one Sunday morning, and afterward one of the patients asked to see me. He was a handsome man, sitting upright in his chair when I entered his room, and he looked right at me.

"Are you the fellow that spoke in the auditorium this morning?" he asked.

"Yes, I am."

"I wasn't there," he told me, "but I heard you on the earphones here by the bed. Tell me about this game of golf, will you? I never did play it."

"You look like a healthy fellow," I replied. "You

should get out there on that little six-hole golf course they have permitted me to install."

I was dumfounded when he said: "Mr. Spence, I'm blind. I have lost my sight completely."

"A great many blind people play golf," I was able to explain. "Why don't you let me teach you?"

"I don't know. They're just now starting to teach me to walk with a cane. But I certainly would like to try if it's possible."

The next day they brought him out at my request. I had a training club with a grip on it where you put your thumbs on the grip of the club and the rest of the fingers fall naturally into place. I also used a ball which, when struck, would swivel around a plastic arm fastened to a spike in the ground. For six weeks I worked with him, along with a group of others, teaching them my four-step system on how to swing the club.

Then one day I told the others that I was going to slip in a real ball on my blind pupil. They all watched silently as I teed it up and then told him to go ahead and swing.

He was using a five iron and he knocked it straight as a string. Those watching applauded vigorously.

"Mr. Spence, you pulled a trick on me," he protested.

"Man," I said, "you just hit that ball 165 yards straight down the middle. I told you that you could play golf."

He had, too, because we measured it. As I said, there's indisputable proof of what blind faith can accomplish.

I have told this story of golf and the Gospel all over the country, but I couldn't use it at a country club.

Why? Because the golf professionals live on giving lesson after lesson and, on the whole, they would pass me off as a religious "nut" for using such a simple method.

Yet the principle is perfect. It is the plan of salvation. Jesus Christ is the answer and the way. I know many people will not believe this simple plan of mine. But I've seen it work. You've got to do it through faith. You eliminate all other thoughts, all the flim-flam business of pronation, and turning, and the 300 pages of gripping a golf club, and the forty things to do taking it back and bringing it forward.

Remember, you are using a God-made thing to swing a golf club. When you take that God-made thing and get up and walk across the room, what do you think of? You see a desk, or a table. The first thing that comes into your mind is: "I see that desk and need something from it. There's the table. I need something from it."

If you broke down every move and tried to get to that table and to that desk by plotting every move, you would fall down and break your leg. Yet you do it easily because each move is automatic.

All I know is that my system works, and it works through faith. As it says in Matthew 17:20:

"For verily I say unto you, If ye have faith as a grain of mustard seed, ye shall say unto this mountain, Remove hence to yonder place; and it shall remove; and nothing shall be impossible unto you."

With Lee Ann Meriwether, Miss America, 1955, and H. C. Ross, of the American Motors Corporation, at the Celebrities Golf Championship, Washington, D.C.

10

But if the watchman see the sword come, and blow not the trumpet, and the people be not warned; if the sword come, and take any person from among them, he is taken away in his iniquity; but his blood will I require at the watchman's hand.
Ezekiel 33:6

The Nineteenth Hole

Two friends of mine drove to the Gator Bowl football game in Jacksonville, Florida, at the end of December, 1963. They stayed at the Roosevelt Hotel and decided to get up early the morning after the game and drive home.

That following day when they left their room, there was a cloud of smoke in the corridor.

"Hey," said one with immediate concern, "there must be a fire somewhere in the hotel."

The other was impatient. "C'mon, c'mon, let's get out

of here and beat the traffic. Somebody else will report it, if there is a fire. Anyhow, they probably have already. So let's not get jammed up here."

The first one nodded ready agreement and, having already checked out, they made a mad dash for their car and headed unconcernedly for home.

Not many miles up the road they turned on the radio in their automobile. They were startled to hear of the conflagration that was sweeping the hotel from which they had departed without worrying about their fellow men who might not have known about the fire.

Twenty-one people died in that blazing holocaust. Sixty other persons were injured, some of whom have not recovered completely to this day.

I do not say that if my friends had sounded an alarm they might have altered what happened in any way. Maybe already it was too late. Probably it wasn't.

But I do say that on the whole we take too casual an attitude about our life and other people's lives. This is one of the reasons that I feel compelled to go forth and help others who, I sincerely believe, may be saved from trials and tribulations I was able to endure and eliminate with God's help. It is entirely possible, I feel, that this is why I was put upon this earth.

In the process there have been times when I have been called a religious fanatic. Knowing what I know, this does not bother me a trifle if, in the process, I can help one lost soul find the right path.

I say to those who scoff and scorn, read, if you dare, the words in the thirty-third chapter of Ezekiel, verses one to six, which I feel are so important in a calloused

world that they should be shouted from the housetops:
"Again the word of the Lord came unto me, saying,

"Son of man, speak to the children of thy people, and
say unto them, when I bring the sword upon a land, if
the people of the land take a man of their coasts, and
set him for their watchman:

"If when he seeth the sword come upon the land, he
blow the trumpet, and warn the people;

"Then whosoever heareth the sound of the trumpet,
and taketh not warning; if the sword come, and take
him away, his blood shall be upon his own head.

"He heard the sound of the trumpet, and took not
warning; his blood shall be upon him. But he that
taketh warning shall deliver his soul.

"But if the watchman see the sword come, and blow
not the trumpet, and the people be not warned; if the
sword come, and take any person from among them, he
is taken away in his iniquity; but his blood will I require at the watchman's hand."

That is the reason, as an alcoholic and drug addict
raised from the abyss by God's word, I will travel to
the ends of the world if I can stay the sword from even
one of my fellow men.

Many times, as we go into various towns and
churches, we are barraged with a wide assortment of
questions concerning alcoholism, drug addiction, and
the theory that they are diseases. I say they are not
diseases.

The only reason I can make this statement, and I
qualify it by saying that I am not a real alcoholic, not
a real drug addict, is that what happened to me was

that I was committing a sin against a holy thing, the temple of God, which is holy. I know this. Read it for yourself, in I Corinthians 3:16–17: "Know ye not that ye are the temple of God, and that the Spirit of God dwelleth in you?

"If any man defile the temple of God, him shall God destroy; for the temple of God is holy, which temple ye are."

Read also I Corinthians 6:19–20, which says: "What? know ye not that your body is the temple of the Holy Ghost which is in you, which ye have of God, and ye are not your own?

"For ye are bought with a price: therefore glorify God in your body, and in your spirit, which are God's."

Thus, if you believe the Bible, your body is a holy temple. Therefore, if we treat it in an unholy manner, and we get sick and die, who can we blame? We cook up a few excuses. We say alcoholism. We say drug addiction. Then, in man's pitifully frail manner, we try to fight these evil and unholy appetites with earthly rationalization. But if we believe that God created us, who are we to fight him?

Did you ever see a clay pot talking back to the potter who made it? The potter molds the clay in his manner. We, as the clay of this earth, through lack of faith are trying to tell the potter who is God how to run his business. We attempt to justify these horrible devices which we visit upon ourselves by saying that they are diseases.

Who ever heard of rape being a disease? Bank robbery? Murder? Are they diseases? I think not. You must classify any of them as a sin because there is a Commandment, "Thou shalt not kill." And if we disintegrate our bodies and minds, even if it be in a slow manner, one which is not immediate but which is a progressive thing, it still must be regarded as a deadly, killing sin.

I was in a church recently in Detroit for services and, when they were over, I was invited to dinner at the minister's home. I was extremely tired because I had been speaking at many places: churches, hospitals, jails, and wherever else I thought I might be able to aid in the Lord's work. But this minister was a dear friend of mine and I went to be with him.

He had invited several others for a late snack, including the chairman of the board of deacons and the latter's young son, a lad of about thirteen. I was asked to give prayer and I did, briefly, because I was mighty tired and the Lord knew it. I had a morning clinic to give early the next day for one of the major motor companies, and I could hardly keep my eyes open.

We had just begun to eat when the chairman of the board of deacons addressed me rather brusquely. "Johnny, don't you think you went rather heavy on the alcohol end of your talk there tonight?"

I sat there a moment, wondering why the chairman of the board of deacons should ask me a question such as that. "What do you mean, sir, that I went a little heavy on alcoholism?"

The question in my mind wasn't long being answered because someone else spoke up and informed me, "The deacon believes that it's all right to take a sociable drink. He does it and it's good for business."

As I say, I was tired. And his testy manner bothered me, too. "Well, sir, whose business is it good for, and what is social drinking? Did I talk about that tonight? I can't remember talking about sociable drinking."

The chairman of the board of deacons scowled across the table and said, "I don't see anything wrong with it."

"Maybe not," I replied, rather curtly, I'm afraid, "but that's a helluva way to look at it."

From the wide-eyed looks cast at me, I knew I had startled everybody at the table.

"I don't mean anything irreverent at all," I told them. "God knows that. But it simply is the brutal truth that I've lived the hell part of it. If I tell you about hell, then I'm going to have to get pretty rough. And that's what drinking has meant to me. There's no way that you can call drinking 'social' and pretend that God sanctions it, because he doesn't. There's no way you can justify sin. Maybe you'll do it. But you can't justify it in God's sight. He may forgive you for it, but he will never justify you."

There was a general clearing of throats and the deacon argued, "I just can't see how I can take one or two drinks and become an alcoholic."

Pointing toward his son, I asked, "Sir, what is that your son is drinking?"

"It's a Seven-Up."

"Well," I told him sharply, "I noticed a whole case of it back there in the kitchen when I came through the back door. I'll tell you what we can do. We'll take all of those drinks and we'll bring 'em in here one at a time and let your boy drink each and every one of those drinks. It doesn't make sense, does it? He may get sick. But unless one drink of alcohol is added he'll only be a Seven-Up-aholic. Unless one drink of alcohol is added, believe me and believe God first, he can never become an alcoholic. He can't become addicted to alcohol unless you first put it in his system. If he never preconditions his mind and his body with liquor, the fact of the matter is that it simply can't ever hurt him."

There was a moment's silence but I wasn't done.

"Sir, you are trying to justify in your eyes the taking of a drink of whiskey, what you call a sociable highball, because it helps your business. Well, let me tell you what God says, and not what John Spence says, and you can read it yourself in Habakkuk 2:15, where it tells you, 'Woe unto him that giveth his neighbour drink, that puttest thy bottle to him, and makest him drunken also, that thou mayest look on their nakedness!' "

It was clearly evident from the scowl on the deacon's face that he was taking this as a personal affront. But, believing the way I believe, I had to tell him what I thought and I kept right on talking.

"God says why don't you then drink, for thou art filled with shameful glory. You are bragging about something that is a shameful thing in God's sight. You asked these things, brother, and I'm going to tell you as it says in Habakkuk 2:16, 'Let thy foreskin be uncovered: the cup of the Lord's right hand shall be turned unto thee, and shameful spewing shall be on thy glory.' So follow me out here tomorrow to the hospital, or to the Rescue Mission in town and see some of these pitiful wrecks, and then try to come back here and tell me again what you have been saying. No, brother, any time you find that God says no and man says yes, you'll find out that man has taken on God's glory. I can't go along with you."

There was complete silence in the room, and a lot of downcast eyes. But not his.

"I don't make a lot of friends," I told him, looking him straight in the eye, "but I have to take God's word for it, and I don't see how any man can stand up and call God a liar and still call himself a Christian. I have a good friend who is a colored minister in the South, and he summed it up for me when he said, 'Mr. Spence, you either is or you isn't for God.'"

I dropped it there. We finished that meal quickly and in silence. There were rather abrupt goodbyes and I went up to bed. Maybe I'll never be invited back there. But that's my stand and I refuse to retreat. It's right there in the Book. Read and understand what it says in Acts 8:20-21:

"Thy money perish with thee, because thou hast thought that the gift of God may be purchased with money.

"Thou hast neither part nor lot in this matter: for thy heart is not right in the sight of God."

That night proved to me that true understanding, as well as faith, is needed desperately throughout the world. In testimony, I can remember the day I went to the towering United Nations building in New York City in company with a small group, and we were taken on a tour of this expensive exercise in international idiocy.

When the tour ended, the man who had taken charge

of the group said to me, in a tone that conveyed the impression that this quibbling edifice of steel and glass was the total answer to the problems of a troubled world, "Well, Mr. Spence, what do you think of all this?"

I hated to tell him, such was his pomposity and his evident belief that this citadel of conversation could make Christian and infidel bedmates, able to "save" the universe. But I did.

"As long as you asked, I'll tell you how I feel. There are three wonderful Christian men working with me. Now, I think it would make sense if you folks would put Bobby Richardson on the dais, place Ray Berry of the Baltimore Colts in the seat of the Russian delegate, install Jerry Kendall of the Minnesota Twins in the spot occupied by the Albanian Communists and, if I'm not too bold, let me represent all of the outraged, downtrodden and aggrieved nations of the world." He stared at me, unable to find words to interrupt.

"Give us those seats," I continued, "and I'll tell you what you can do with this lovely building. You can take it and convert it into a hospital to serve mankind, because with Christian love we would disassemble your nuclear weapons and bring harmony and peace to the world."

Finally he found his voice, a somewhat startled look on his face. "Where did you ever come up with such reasoning?" he demanded.

"Well," I told him, "just open your Bible, if there's one hidden somewhere among all your law books and political tracts, and read II Chronicles 7:14. For there it says, 'If my people, which are called by my name, shall humble themselves, and pray, and seek my face, and turn from their wicked ways; then will I hear from heaven, and will forgive their sin, and will heal their land.' "

He still looked a bit shaken and confused when I said goodbye and left. Such is the state of this bickering, bloodthirsty world that brotherly love has been lost in the tumultuous flood of international avarice and conflicting isms, and even the voices of those who speak for God are drowned out by the raucous roars of those preaching hate and conquest.

Yet this wayward path away from the Lord is noticeable in all walks of life and, I am sorry to say, particularly in sports, where those who should be shining examples for the youth of the land betray this trust in staggering numbers.

Baseball, as an example, has been littered with bottle men. Some of these bibulous roisterers I knew extremely well. While they are to blame for the image they create, there is small cause for wondering why, when you take into account that the major league teams themselves receive most of their television advertising revenue from beer and cigarettes, putting their greed ahead of the impression these commercials are making on the hero-worshiping youngsters who are baseball fans. Isn't it a shame, and a sad commentary on our way of life, that you never hear of a dairy company sponsoring baseball games? Professional football was shocked when "Big Daddy" Lipscomb, one of its outstanding stars, reputedly died from an overdose of narcotics, and yet a number of its talented players have been noted tipplers.

Golf, through the very nature of the game, has always had more than its share of alcoholic casualties. The "nineteenth hole" symbolizes internationally the constant, never-ending bouts with John Barleycorn. The bar in the men's locker room and the "grill room" (where mostly people are "fried") are the favorite spots for "relaxation" after a round of play.

Don't imagine that I am stretching a point. Maybe there are people who can be "sociable" drinkers, although I doubt it, for alcohol seemed always to create a Jekyll-Hyde metamorphosis in just about everyone I ever knew. But even if there are such people, the liquid society of the nineteenth hole treads a perilous tightrope across a bottomless quagmire because the hairline marking the boundary to alcoholism is a nebulous thing.

A case in point came on an occasion when I spoke at a mission in Chicago's Tenderloin district. These were broken men, there primarily for a handout; bums such as I had been the night I almost died. I feel no repugnance for such as these, for I was one of them, and my heart goes out to them with a vast pity. I told them that they were not beyond redemption if only they would come back to God, and described to them in detail how I had found the way. Then I read to them from John 3:16: "For God so loved the world, that he gave his only begotten Son, that whosoever believeth in him should not perish, but have everlasting life."

When I had finished, one of those human bits of flotsam, a man who looked as if he had lived in the gutter all his life, shambled forward. There were tears in his eyes when he spoke to me.

"Johnny, you couldn't possibly remember me, but I remember you."

"Where was that, brother?"

He wiped his eyes and nose on a tattered sleeve. "I met you during the All America World's Championship at the Tam O'Shanter Country Club," he said, naming one of the most famous clubs in the Chicago area. "I was a member there, had a fine job, made lots of money, and had a wonderful family. But it's all gone now, job, money and family. I got started playing gin rummy and drinking in the locker room every day. I'm one of those guys who couldn't handle it, an alcoholic who didn't think it could ever happen to me. But it did."

Sobs racked his body and he gasped through his tears, "Johnny, I want to find my way back. I want the life you've been talking about. Please help me."

"There's no reason you can't have all those wonderful things again if you will go back to God, just as I did," I comforted him.

Then, trying to give him time to recover his composure, I told him to listen as I read to him from I Peter 5:6-7: "'Humble yourselves therefore under the mighty hand of God, that he may exalt you in due time:

"'Casting all your care upon him; for he careth for you.'"

We were able to help this man, praise the Lord, and once again he is a respected member of his community.

Too many times, however, they lose the way and never regain it. There is a picture on the wall of a midwestern golf club today showing a man held high on the shoulders of a crowd, and in his hand is a highball. This man once was my idol when I was a young professional and I had the opportunity to play a round with him.

I'm referring to Cyril Walker, who defeated Bobby Jones at Oakland Hills Country Club in Birmingham, Michigan, in 1924, to win the coveted United States Open golf championship. A few years passed and Cyril Walker vanished from the public eye. It was as if he had never inhabited the earth, this fine golfer who had won the biggest prize the game has to offer. Such is fame that one day there was a small item tucked in the corner of the newspaper: Cyril Walker had died alone in the jail of a small town in New Jersey from acute alcoholism.

Actually the hazards of the golf tour increase annually for those who are living in glamour, glory, and the close conformity of a world interested principally in the material things of life. As golf grows larger and ever larger, those who are its top performers become more and more in demand in the liquid atmosphere of country club life.

They forget that there is a passage in the Bible which says there is a way that seems right to man, but the end of that way is the way of death.

There was another great golfing champion who quit the game when he was in his early forties because, some said, he didn't want to play second fiddle. Walker was a man who gloried in his reputation as a great drinker. Yet you can look in the opposite direction at

a man such as Sam Snead, who takes care of himself
physically, never drank or smoked, and returned to golf,
remaining a winner even into his fifties. No false pride
there, for while everyone said he never could win the
U. S. Open because he finished second four times and
it had to have become a mental block, Sam still was
never too proud to appear and take his chances.

The other man's vanity wouldn't let him try when he
knew he couldn't win. And the Bible speaks, too, of
that. For in Proverbs 16:18 it tells us: "Pride goeth before destruction, and an haughty spirit before a fall."

I had not attended a major golfing event for some
time when I went to the Doral Country Club in Miami
a couple of years back. While there, I had lunch with
Billy Maxwell, a fine young man from Texas and a wonderful player I had known for years, and Jacky Cupit,
who had arrived on the tour after I left.

We were having a sandwich and I bowed my head
and solemnly thanked God that I could be there in a
place of conformity, being in the world and not of it, not
through any power of my own, but through the trans-
forming power of an almighty, all-powerful, all-loving
God.

Billy asked me to tell him about what I was doing.
Now I have long since made it a practice never to tell
people unless they ask me. If you do, they feel as if
you are trying to force your beliefs and ideals upon
them. So I pray for discernment, and I trust that God
will never let me make this way of life look offensive to
anyone, even though it is a way which God has shown
to me to be the right way. Only through love and kind-

ness can we ever show a person how God really feels about him.

I told them of my feelings and my work, and both showed great interest. Then the talk turned again to golf and Billy said, "I saw you going up and down the practice range. What do you think of the swings?"

"They're actually no better than they were ten years ago," I told him. "It's like a Christian life, Billy. It isn't how you swing, it's the desire of the individual."

They were amused when I told them that when Arnold Palmer broke in on the tour, I was asked many times whether he was any relation to Johnny Palmer. Johnny was a fine golfer out of the South who won many tournaments and was defeated by Sam Snead in the finals of the 1949 P.G.A. championship at Hermitage Country Club in Richmond, Virginia. While they were not related, both of them played in the Masters in 1955, Arnold's first time as a professional, and I had him on a television program at station WRDW in Augusta.

We chatted awhile longer and then, when we walked outside near the putting green, Billy pointed to one of golf's greatest "names" and asked me, "What do you think is wrong with him that he can't win any more?" This man had won them all, and now he couldn't finish in the money.

"I'll tell you what I think is wrong with him," I replied.

I related that I had been at Oakland Hills in 1961 when Gene Littler won the U. S. Open championship, merely stopping by before speaking at a youth meeting

in Detroit. Cobby Ware, a ministerial student at that
time, was talking to me, and he frowned in thought and
said to me, "Mr. Spence, I saw a picture of you someplace that was made right here at Oakland Hills."

"Well, that was exactly ten years ago, in 1951, when
Ben Hogan won the championship. Then I was one of
the glad boys in the bar and was treated as a celebrity
who had the run of the grounds. My open-air golf shop
was the center of attraction and I made a couple of
thousand dollars that week. Today I stand here and
hardly anybody recognizes me, but I'm happier than
I've ever been in my life."

I related all this to Billy Maxwell and then picked
up the theme of the big man to whom he had pointed.
"While I was talking to Cobby, that fellow came over
to me and asked, 'Johnny, where have you been keeping yourself? I haven't seen you in years. Come in and
have lunch with me.' "

I told Billy how I had explained to this man that I
was only on the course and grounds because I was
wearing my P.G.A. badge, but that I didn't have a
clubhouse pass.

"You come in as my guest and nobody will say anything," he asserted.

So I went to lunch with this man who soon was to
tee off in the United States Open and he ordered: "A
double martini."

Then he turned back to me and confessed, "Johnny,
I just don't seem to be able to play any more. I haven't
even been close to winning a tournament in a couple of
years, and I can't figure out what's wrong. I'm just having all sorts of trouble and it makes me sick."

At which point he ordered another double martini.

"But how about you?" he asked suddenly. "You know, Johnny, the first golf tournament I won, right after the war when balls were still impossible to get, you gave me three balls and I won with them. I've never forgotten it. I heard you've been sick. Is there anything I can do to help you?"

I didn't answer him right away. Because I sat there looking at this man, thinking of the money he had and the position he had attained, and how he was dissipating everything, and I felt a tremendous compassion and love for him. My pocketbook was mighty thin, actually flat, and yet I was much better off than he, because I knew that what he was doing right that minute was the cause of his problems.

Two double martinis in the middle of the day, before he set out in the first round of the United States Open!

"That's wonderful of you," I finally replied, "but let me ask you something, pardner. You tell me you're not winning. What's your trouble?"

"Well, a lot of things. I've had an ulcer and actually a little family trouble. My mother-in-law has been interfering with my home life, and my marriage isn't exactly on solid ground."

He gave me several other reasons for his golf game being bad, but he never did hit on the real one.

That martini he had in his hand—in the middle of the day, when he was about to go out into the hot sun, under great pressure, and when he would need full control of his muscles and every one of his senses—was the basis of all his difficulties.

At first I couldn't open my mouth to this man of

whom I thought so much and to whom I wanted to speak so badly. Finally it came.

"Pardner, you know I had trouble. You asked me what it was. Well, mine was the very thing you're holding in your right hand."

"This?" he scoffed incredulously, twirling the martini around in its glass. "Johnny, this doesn't bother me a bit. You know I can handle it. I can take it or leave it alone."

"Well, did you ever think that maybe you'd play a little better if you left it alone?"

"Johnny, all I wanted to do was to settle my nerves. I had an argument with my wife when I left today, and . . . well, hell, this will help much more than it could possibly hurt me."

Billy Maxwell and Jacky Cupit stood there wide-eyed while I told them this story and ended it lamely by adding, "My heart bled for this man because I knew that there was no chance that he would see it my way. And yet, there was the reason for his big skid, right there in that martini glass he held in his hand."

Blame it on the pressures of the tour, if you will. They all hope to stay on the top, even though the time must come when they have been long at the peak and must start down. Yet still they rush the downhill process, not because God would have them do so, but because of their way of life. There are parties every night which they feel they must attend and, while they can stand up to it for a while, sooner or later it must have a telling effect. Pressures, yes, but if they walked with God there can be no question but that their golden years would be extended. Yet how do you get this across to them?

There are enough hazards without looking for them. The golf professionals travel constantly, which in itself is a risky business. Take the case of Ben Hogan, who, after winning his first United States Open in 1948, was almost killed the winter of 1949 in a collision with a bus in Texas. Dottie and I came along shortly afterward and saw the results of that accident. How, we wondered, did he and his wife Valerie survive?

God has his purpose, I suppose, as he does in everyone's life. For Ben came back to win many championships through his courage, ability, and championship qualities; and yet he was grateful enough to give God the credit.

Those in charge held a dinner for Ben at the Celebrities tournament in Washington when he was making his comeback in 1950 and, while he was thin and seemingly still very weak, he stood up there at the microphone with sportscaster Harry Wismer and said, "I would like to give thanks to my friends around the world for their prayers that helped me fight my way back."

Right afterward at Merion Golf Club in Ardmore, Pennsylvania, he won the second of his four United States Open championships that put him in a tie with the immortal Bobby Jones and Willie Anderson for the most total victories in this great championship.

This isn't an isolated case, either. Skip Alexander, a very dear friend of ours, missed his plane connection after one tournament and was given a ride in a Civil Air

Patrol plane. It crashed in Evansville, Indiana, and the plane caught fire. The others died. Skip, horribly burned, broke his way out of the plane and somehow managed to crawl away from the flaming wreckage.

Shortly thereafter, I was scheduled to leave for the annual P.G.A. meeting in Chicago. Dottie baked a cake for Skip, with a tiny figure of a golfer on it, and I carried it carefully on the train to Evansville. When I arrived at the Lutheran Hospital there and was led to his room, I didn't recognize him. I walked out into the hall filled with emotion and—imagine it!—his wife consoled me, telling me that he was a fighter and with God's help would live.

He did, and battled his way back to golf, which is a tribute to him. But, as in Hogan's case, the prayers of many, many people had to have helped him to an extent which is immeasurable. Miracles such as these, and they were miracles that both Ben and Skip lived, don't just happen. They occur because God wills them and, in his infinite mercy, grants the supplications of those who are in his fold.

I am forced to hold that sports is the branch of life which I know the best and yet, the further I go in the field of faith which has been granted to me, the more I realize that every walk of life is beset with the very same problems.

Not long ago I was called on to speak at a penitentiary, and I gave it to them straight from the shoulder.

"The only difference between you men sitting out there in uniforms and me up here with a business suit on is that this suit was given to me by some of God's people. I wear it, too, only with the grace of God, or maybe I'd be sitting out there with you," I admitted. "But that grace of his is more than enough, and I must be here because God wanted you to have this conversion experience, which is a personal thing that must be done with the heart, soul, and mind of the individual."

When it was over the warden told me that a young prisoner wanted to talk to me.

"Mr. Spence," said this fine-looking young fellow, "I can't ever imagine you hitting the bottle. You know, I caddied for you in Reading, Pennsylvania, one time, and you were a real big shot. You had a big car and you were a heavy tipper. I just can't imagine you taking drugs and winding up busted out."

I looked him right in the eye. "Well, son, I told you about it and that's the way it happened. Now tell me, what happened to you?"

He looked down at the floor, and his young face creased into hard, bitter lines. Then he started to talk, forcibly, as if he couldn't wait to get it out, and I didn't interrupt him.

"When I caddied for you I was in high school. I was a football player and a good one. I thought about going to college on a scholarship, and I know I would have made good because I wasn't only the biggest in my class but I was at the top scholastically, too.

"Now I never smoked or drank, Mr. Spence, but I used to go down to the corner poolroom and hang around there with the fellows. One night a guy came in there who we all had seen around the neighborhood and thought was some kind of a big shot because he had a foreign car and always dressed real sharp. So this night he walks in and asks who was the biggest and strongest guy in the joint. He said he needed somebody to drive him that night because he was gonna get drunk and wanted somebody who could handle him.

"We all were kind of tongue-tied, but he laid a twenty-dollar bill up on one of the pool tables. I'd never had a twenty-dollar bill in my life, so I walked up, looked it over to make sure it was legit, and stuck it in my pocket. 'I'm your boy,' I told him.

"I'm talkin' too much, Mr. Spence, but before the night was over I'd had my first drink of liquor, I took part in a holdup, and I killed a policeman with a gun this man had given me.

"Now," he said, breathlessly, "I'm in for life."

What heartbreak. You can see signs on any highway advertising beer and whiskey. Why doesn't someone put up signs on the roadsides showing a picture of this young man and what alcohol did to him?

The warden told me, before I left, that 71 per cent of those to whom I had talked in that penitentiary were there for crimes for which they had preconditioned their bodies and their minds with wine, beer or whiskey. Imagine it, more than seven out of every ten!

On another occasion, I was privileged to speak at the oldest Methodist church in America, the John Street Church in the Wall Street district of New York City. One of those who came up after the service to give his life to God through Christ was an airline pilot who held the record for an east-to-west crossing of the Atlantic.

"I pushed that plane almost beyond its capabilities

for only one reason," he admitted. "I could hardly wait to get home and get a drink."

Several years later I saw him again and he was glowing with health, whole again, and happy. And I thought with rejoicing of what it says in Luke 17:19: "And he said unto him, Arise, go thy way: thy faith hath made thee whole."

That day, as we left the church, I stopped at the corner and bought a paper from a newsboy. There, in big black letters, it told how motion-picture star Diana Barrymore had been found dead in an apartment littered with empty whiskey and pill bottles.

My mind flashed back to a night when Dottie and I had been invited to a party in Hollywood during my days of distress, and how I had sat and talked with the "Too Much, Too Soon" girl. She was drinking champagne and I was drinking anything in sight.

"My father and most of our family all have been natural drinkers," she told me. "I guess you'd have to say I just inherited the talent."

All of it came back to me as I stood there on that sidewalk in New York with people hurrying past, and I thought that this woman died because she played a game more dangerous than Russian roulette. In her case, all of the chambers of the gun were loaded.

A similarly distressing case was that of little Gail Russell, another of those we met in Hollywood. She had parted from her family, spent days on end drinking in her room alone, and was found dead. Who wants to die like that?

Yet how many times have I heard people say, "Ah,

you can quit it if you want to. It's all a mental thing."

So they put us in mental institutions, and you can try to figure out the tragedy of that. They advertise it, they sell it, and then they tell you you're crazy if you drink it. On top of this, it is these same people who think that we who go with God are peculiar, and are eager to throw rocks at us.

I can tell you this in all truth, because I've been the target often since I saw the light. But I know that the love of God through Christ is sufficient to keep me going. He didn't say he would give me everything I wanted. He said he would give me above what I needed. For a man who has been out of work as long as I, and who still keeps gaining weight, I have to believe without equivocation that God is truly sufficient.

No one has to tell me that it is all too easy to walk the way of conformity. Satan had a headlock on me for too long for me not to know that most of us have almost irresistible appetites to touch, feel, taste, have, and own.

Not even all of those who profess themselves to be true Christians are innocent. Many of those who profess Christianity the loudest go to church merely to be seen as pillars of the community. On the outside they are beyond reproach, wearing the Sunday suit, the Sunday expression, the Sunday personality.

Catch those same guys on Monday and you'll see who they really are, disguising their cheating, lying, drinking and swindling under the all-inclusive guise of "business." Too few are those who totally dedicate their life to the godly principles which are right and righteous, whole and holy.

This point was hammered home even to me, one of the worst of sinners, when I spoke to a group of young people in Dallas at one of the richest churches in the world. My life was for years a grim affair, and I would be remiss in my duty to God if I didn't tell even the young people of the pitfalls life has to offer, and hold myself up as an example of that which is to be shunned. So I told them of the downward path and the degradation. And I finished by quoting to them from I Corinthians 3:16–17: "Know ye not that ye are the temple of God, and that the spirit of God dwelleth in you?

"If any man defile the temple of God, him shall God destroy; for the temple of God is holy, which temple ye are."

Shortly thereafter I received a letter from a seventeen-year-old girl who had been one of the group to which I had spoken. It began, "Mr. Spence, I just had to sit down and write you a thank-you note."

But then this thank-you "note" turned out to be eight long pages written from a heart already broken at her tender age by tawdry acts which had been forced upon her. The scalding words poured across those pages as if they had been written in her own blood, a missive which ended in sheer pathos:

"Why didn't someone tell me these things you told us, because I and others among our group didn't really know what was going on? Our parents are members of the church. I have wanted all my life to be a true Christian and love in the way which God sets up, but it is true that the outside world wouldn't let me live that way."

So you may say, as many do, that people such as these are no affair of mine. But I believe it is God's will that they are and should be. It comes to me from Genesis 4:9–11:

"And the Lord said unto Cain, Where is Abel thy brother? And he said, I know not: Am I my brother's keeper?

"And he said, What hast thou done? the voice of thy brother's blood crieth unto me from the ground.

"And now art thou cursed from the earth, which hath opened her mouth to receive thy brother's blood from thy hand."

Inmates at South Carolina State Penitentiary, 1964, getting a Spence golf lesson. Bible is in the foreground.

11

Remember the sabbath day, to keep it holy.
Six days shalt thou labor, and do all thy work: But the seventh day is the sabbath of the Lord thy God: in it thou shalt not do any work, thou, nor thy son, nor thy daughter, thy manservant, nor thy maidservant, nor thy cattle, nor thy stranger that is within thy gates.   *Exodus 20:8–10*

The Sunday Problem

Read those last eight words above particularly well, digest them, and take them to your heart.

". . . nor thy stranger that is within thy gates."

The touring golf professionals who must play on Sunday are strangers "within thy gates," whether a tournament is held in San Francisco or Sandusky, Miami or Martha's Vineyard.

Many times, as I go around the United States, I must tell people that I am the only member of the Professional Golfers Association of America that I know of who is unemployed, because of my stand against Sunday golf.

I have been rejected because I hold, without equivocation, that if you are a Christian then you should not play golf on Sunday, you should not teach golf on Sunday, and you should not even attend a tournament on a Sunday. To me it is the Lord's day and must belong completely to him without any other interests whatsoever.

Few tournament professionals and hardly any club professionals get to go to church on Sunday. Yet, as the Christian world knows, God made heaven and earth in six days. Read for yourself in Genesis 2:2–3 what he says again of the Sabbath: "And on the seventh day God ended his work which he had made; and he rested on the seventh day from all his work which he had made.

"And God blessed the seventh day, and sanctified it: because that in it he had rested from all his work which God created and made."

My stand today is that if almighty God, the creator of this earth, the galaxies, the stars, the moon and the heavens and the oceans, if he rested on one day, then why did he do it? Why? He wanted to be glorified on this day, and he has given us many, many reasons why we should take the Sabbath and make it holy.

Many people say that here's a fellow over here who is taking this day, or that day. God said the Sabbath day is a holy day. He meant for us to have a time of meditation. To do these things even as Jesus did. And he is so specific that one day out of seven should be

given to glorify him and his son that he tells us throughout the Bible how he blessed this one day out of the
week.

I intend here to explain fully why I feel all golf
courses should be used as much as possible through the
six days—and not on the Sabbath. Listen to what God
says in Isaiah 58:13 if you are in doubt: "If thou turn
away thy foot from the sabbath, from doing thy pleasure on my holy day; and call the sabbath a delight, the
holy of the Lord, honourable; and shalt honour him, not
doing thine own ways, nor finding thine own pleasure,
nor speaking thine own words."

It has to be obvious that, where Sunday is concerned,
he isn't pulling any punches. Neither will I. This is a
holy day, not a holiday; a day of devotion, not a day of
desecration.

I know that people go fishing, boating, and hunting,
in addition to playing or watching golf. But I know golf.
This has been my life. And it was because of the necessity of conforming to the world of golf as a young man
that I turned away from my mother's pleadings to give
up something for God.

Now I do not believe that we can take one hour of his
day to honor him and use the remaining hours of that
day to desecrate him. The Professional Golfers Association has never attempted to follow the example which
was set for it long ago by the United States Golf Association. For money it even permits a whiskey company
to put on its senior championship.

And now the United States Golf Association, which

prided itself for so long as the guiding organization that guarded the ideals of golf in this country, has, through greed, surrendered its shield and buckler.

Why? Not for the Almighty, but for the almighty dollar. Because in 1965 it finally capitulated and extended the United States Open golf tournament over four days.

Up until then the United States Golf Association, an amateur body with no need of vast funds, scheduled the United States Open championship over three days, with one round on Thursday, one round on Friday, and two rounds on Saturday to finish it up. This is as it should be done.

Yet, while preserving its face, the United States Golf Association wavered, too. For whenever there was a tie in the championship, the playoff was run on Sunday. They had, of course, an "out" against the protests of religious dissenters: they hadn't scheduled the event for Sunday.

Still, whenever there was a tie they were contributing to the desecration of the Lord's day.

Don't let them tell you they couldn't have kept Sunday open and operated the playoff on Monday. Of course they could. Because only the two or three players involved in the tie would have been forced to remain on the scene. Thus they all could have honored the Lord's day of rest. Tournament golfers are working men. They, too, deserve this demanded day of rest, and the opportunity to respect the day of devotion.

But it simply was more profitable to the United States Golf Association to hold its playoff on Sunday because on this "non-working day" they could draw a larger crowd than they could on Monday.

They forgot what it says in Ephesians 4:19: "Who being past feeling have given themselves over unto lasciviousness, to work all uncleanness with greediness."

The United States Golf Association claimed that it was forced to do this and have the playoff on Sunday. I say it is not necessary or true, due to the very fact that each year the prize money has increased as golf became more and more of a spectator sport, increasing even in years when there was no playoff on Sunday. They were not suffering financially, and there was absolutely no need to hold the playoff on the Sabbath.

Prior to instituting the Sunday playoff, the United States Golf Association, when it was formed just prior to the turn of the century and was striving to become the guiding force in the game, never permitted play on Sunday.

They remembered, as they should today, that one of the founding principles of this great country of ours was to provide and secure freedom of worship. To worship what? Certainly not golf. But gradually they infringed on the Sabbath under the guise of its being necessary to finish up a tied tournament by getting the playoff out of the way.

Who was in a hurry? Certainly not the competitors, who could have used God's day of rest. Certainly not the United States Golf Association. For it has been on the scene since its organization in 1894 and at this late date doesn't have to be in a rush to get anywhere.

It was greed. And this was proved in 1965 when it

made its decision to extend the final round to Sunday instead of holding the two closing rounds on Saturday. Now there is not even the sham pretense of playing on Sunday only when a playoff is necessary.

The United States Golf Association lost moral prestige when it decided that it would alter its format to a four-day tournament just like any other on the professional circuit, playing Thursday, Friday, Saturday—and Sunday.

They had the weak excuse they needed. For in 1964 at Congressional Country Club in Washington, D.C., Ken Venturi won the United States Open in blazing heat which almost caused him to collapse from heat prostration. He needed a doctor's care during the luncheon break between the semifinal and final round on Saturday.

The physical exhaustion factor was seized upon by the United States Golf Association and given as one of its main reasons for ending the two-round finish on Saturday and extending play to single rounds on Saturday and Sunday.

Even Venturi, a godly young man of great faith, spoke forth against this decision.

The United States Golf Association had always contended, in support of its windup two rounds on Saturday, that physical endurance should be a factor in such a great championship. Venturi, along with many others, held that endurance should play a part in winning the United States Open, and objected to extending the tournament over into Sunday.

But television pays large sums for the right to tele-cast the United States Open championship, as well as other major golf tournaments and various other sport-ing events. So the operators of these events cast God aside and bow to the sponsors, who are intent on utiliz-ing Sunday because it is a "big day" on home television. These "Sunday salesmen" work on the theory that they can push their products better because of the larger audience.

This is a farce. If the United States Golf Association said to the networks, "We will hold the playoff on Mon-day so that people can have their day of devotion," that is the way it would have to be. Yet, by capitu-lating, they are helping to keep people away from God's house of worship.

The United States Golf Association, since the days when it was seeking national acceptance, has always patterned itself after the guiding body of golf in Great Britain, namely, the Royal and Ancient.

It and its leaders should look again at those who founded this great game. For the British Open golf championship is not played on the Sabbath and neither, it might be added, is the Canadian Open. They will not surrender God for gold.

I know that by making this statement as a member of the Professional Golfers Association I will come un-der heavy fire from many directions. I am accustomed to this and will not retreat.

As I said, I have been rejected by the few clubs at which I have been offered jobs, because I demanded only to be let off all day on the Lord's day. If I worked at a golf course on Sunday today, I know that the Lord would not bless me.

The Professional Golfers of America could make money, and in abundance, without desecrating Sunday. And what happy homes they would have. I have talked to the wives of many of the players who travel on the tour with their husbands, and I know how many of these fine women who were brought up in religious homes are unhappy because of Sunday tournament play. What they would like is to be able to go to church as a family and use this entire day for the glory of God.

Nor do the players themselves want to give up a quiet and healing Sabbath with their families and their God.

The P.G.A. contends, in winding up virtually every one of its tournaments on Sunday, that this must be done because this is a day when large galleries can come and the all-important gate is large financially.

Personally, I look back with regret on the ten years in which I worked as a partner with Ed Dudley, professional then at the Augusta Masters Golf Club, in his golf shop during the annual Masters golf championship.

Driving to the course on Sunday mornings, my wife and I often were filled with remorse as we saw families walking in close union toward their house of worship. I had, at that time, gotten so far away from God, and had sunk so low, that money was my only thought. Yet, even so, the needle of my conscience would not be completely stilled.

We would drive onto the course to find that thousands and thousands of others had arrived even before us, storming the gates on a day which God set aside to worship his son, while we all were worshiping graven images. Tickets were sold to watch men whose names had been built up for headlines and money, and God wasn't even on the bill.

What can be done? I'll tell you what can be done and what should be done. It is up to all parishioners, to the clergy who are failing in their duty, and to the backsliding Christians of all these desecrated towns and cities, to band together and demand that golf not be allowed to soil their homes and lives on the Sabbath.

As as example, let us consider the city of Augusta, Georgia, where the famous Masters golf championship is run on Thursday, Friday, Saturday—and Sunday.

This, undeniably, is a Christian city. Yet its Sunday crowd is one of the largest ever seen annually at any tournament. So I say that it is up to the people of Augusta to have the intestinal fortitude—what professional athletes call plain "guts"—to take a stand for what God has ordered and make a concerted mass stand for God and family.

God plainly tells us throughout his work that such people shouldn't call themselves a Christian people, they shouldn't call themselves a Christian city, and that theirs should not be called a Christian state while they dishonor God on his day. This holds not only for Augusta but for every city in any state which permits golf on Sunday.

I wonder, as I travel around the country, about these clergymen who stand up in the pulpit and read what I have pointed out here, from Genesis and Isaiah, and yet do nothing but give it lip service instead of combined, concentrated action.

They tell us these things. But notice that they, too, condone—merely by ignoring—golf being played in their town or city on Sunday.

You say how do they condone it when they don't go to it? You're kidding yourself and they are, too. They condone it by not condemning it. They don't go to their members and say, "Listen, let's start a crusade here that this town next year will put up banners, and we will march down the street, a solid mass of Christians, saying let's take a stand against Sunday golf. Let's not permit this desecration of our city."

Everybody is picketing something or other these days. Why then can't we picket for Christ? Why can't the clergymen of Augusta and other cities join together and parade downtown and say, "You who call yourselves Christians, why don't you take a stand and come out here and let's see which side you're on. Will you take a stand for Jesus Christ?"

Remember the song, "Stand Up, Stand Up for Jesus"? How many of them, how many of you, will do it today?

This may well separate you from the conforming crowd. People may point a finger at you. But it's a likely method by which we can get this country back to God. And it is my solid belief, and I will not retreat from my stand, that the clergy are the ones who should lead the way. They are officially the pastors of the flock, and if they believe what they teach, they should trumpet at the forefront of God's legions.

My finding has been, in working with hundreds of ministers across the country, that they're all for it. Except for one thing. They say, "Fine, but Johnny, you do it." They have been naïve and they have been spineless. They have absolutely turned their backs on the obligation they owe to Almighty God.

I believe that many of them, like seventeen-year-old Johnny Spence when he turned his back on God, are afraid for their jobs. They are fearful of what somebody on the board of deacons might say. They flinch from doing the job. They are putting man and his wants before God.

It is bad enough when they so lack faith in God that they send the members of their flocks to psychiatrists and marriage counselors. Yet unless they, as the spiritual leaders, shoulder this obligation, and unless they stride to the fore, who are we to say that Communism is a bad way of life?

Everybody wants to take a stand against something. But there are very few who take a stand *for* something. To take a stand for God's own day means that we have to give up something. God says to give it up, and his word is more important to me than winning the Open, the Masters, or any other tournament you could ever name. I love golf and I honor those who can win those championships, but again I say, they should be won on a Saturday, or a Monday, but never on a Sunday.

I love my fellow professionals, those who are in charge at the Masters, those who head the U.S.G.A., and the leaders of the Professional Golfers Association.

Many of them are wonderful, dear friends of mine. They may well hate me for what I am saying. But there can be no question but that these men who are the leaders should do what God has told us in II Chronicles 7:14.

Do they call themselves Christians? Well, God is going to challenge them, and I'll spell it out right here. He's going to say, if you call yourself a Christian, then prove it to me. For in that verse from II Chronicles he tells us: "If my people, which are called by my name, shall humble themselves, and pray, and seek my face, and turn from their wicked ways; then will I hear from heaven, and will forgive their sin, and will heal their land."

Make your own test. Go out on the street and ask the first person you meet if he is a Christian. The odds are that he'll tell you that he is, of course. Suppose you say to him then, "Did you know this country is about to be taken over by Communism?"

Probably he'd call you, at best, merely an alarmist. But say to him something like this: "Look at Cuba and how close they have moved in. Look at over six hundred million people already under the domination of Communism right now, and it only started less than fifty years ago. We started with Christianity thousands of years ago, and already they've become a challenge."

They're moving mighty fast. We, as Christians, are dragging our feet, seeking the easy way out and forgetting to do as God says. He tells us if we have a problem—and Sunday golf has created a major problem, along with Sunday football, Sunday baseball and other Sabbath distractions—there's one thing he wants us to do. That's to humble ourselves, pray, seek his face, and turn from our wicked ways.

How are we going to humble ourselves? I recently turned down a job that would have paid me $50,000 a year. That's a lot of money. Ten dollars is a lot of money to me now. But I will not turn my back on the Lord's word.

This doesn't make me a hero. It doesn't make me a martyr or place me on a pedestal. But I know how far he can reach, and I know how he can pull you out of the miry clay of sin. He did it for me when he picked me up and placed me back on my feet. He has a mighty long arm. So when God says turn from your wicked ways and I'll forgive your sins, I have to listen.

And what about where he says, "I'll heal your land?" What's the matter with our land? It's the people. You can go out here across the length and breadth of this blessed country and find beautiful grass and magnificent trees on the golf courses. You can find lovely turf out at Yankee Stadium. To football fans nothing is prettier than the green grass of the gridiron.

Yet you'd be surprised how many of the great athletes who must perform on Sunday would rather be in the Lord's house. They are forced to play or be pushed out of the sport.

Recently I talked to one of the greatest golfers I ever knew, a wonderful, devout family man named Mike Souchak. He recalled how I had given him a lift to

church one Sunday morning when, bone-tired, he had
to rush back to make his starting time in the closing
round of a golf tournament.

Mike Souchak put God first, but necessity drove him
back to the golf course when he should have had that
whole day to rest and be with his family and his God.
Mike simply can't change the format as much, I am
quite certain, as he would love to see it changed.

It's up to those who call themselves God's children.
They can force promoters and golf officials to finish
tournaments on Saturdays instead of Sundays. I was on
the tour for ten years, and I can tell you that we were
rained out on many Sundays. Yet the tournament came
back the next year just as if nothing had happened to
force a Sunday postponement the year before. Sunday
play is merely a gimmick of the greedy who think they
can make a few more dollars.

I work with young Bobby Richardson, the second
baseman of the New York Yankees. I work with Ray-
mond Berry, an all-time great from Southern Methodist
University, who plays end for the Baltimore Colts professional football team. Also with Jerry Kendall of the
Minnesota Twins, and a lot of other wonderful Christian boys.

They tell me how they'd love to see Sunday set aside
as the Lord's day. But they are merely players on a team
run by people who are putting God second, third, or
last.

How do we explain away the fact that wonderful
boys such as these still play on Sunday? They must. It
isn't a sport with them. They are men with families for

whom they must make a living, and it is all too well known in sports that those at the top don't last very long as time is measured. But to them it is purely and simply a job and, while they love the game they play, they don't cherish playing it on Sunday.

In summarizing this Sunday problem, I must come back and assert that basically it is the clergy who are at fault. Those who call themselves the shepherds of the flock have let God down. If these men in the pulpit would get up and tell the deacons, the elders, and the congregations, "This we must do," then God would help them get it done.

Let them admit that it is a stand which may lose them their positions, but let them tell the Christian world that in the Bible God says we are to keep this holy day not for an hour, not for thirty minutes at Sunday school, but that this is the "day" which should be kept holy. And if they joined together in truly holy union, their power, like that of the Lord, would be all-conquering.

It is they who should take a united stand, advising the world that each one wants his church to become a solid rock in God's citadel. But I feel that some of these men who are preaching Jesus Christ cannot believe in him. They may deny my assertion, and yet they're going to have to prove it to me from the Bible. How can they preach on Easter morning that Jesus Christ has risen, and then by silence condone their flock's going to a golf tournament in the afternoon? Such a man is not a leader but merely a worldly man preaching in sonorous tones and leaving us hanging by the thumbs in the air.

They are the ones who must put their feet down and take a solid stand for God. If the clergy and the National Council of Churches, the American Baptist Convention, the Southern Baptist Convention, and all other church organizations firmly took this stand, I can assure you that the United States Golf Association, the Masters golf tournament, and the P.G.A., all would be forced to move in accordance.

For with the combined strength of these organizations it would be as it says in Judges 20:8: "All the people arose as one man."

I feel very deeply about the sacrilege which is Sunday golf.

Of course, not playing golf on Sunday, and refusing to attend a tournament on Sunday, will not get me into heaven. The only manner in which I am saved is by God's grace.

Yet, if the Christians of the world banded together under a militant leadership—militant for God—a dent could be made somewhere. Somewhere, under a concerted drive by men of faith, Sunday golf could be eliminated. One hole in the dike is all that is needed, for then the Christian peoples of this nation would rise up on a national scale and see that every tournament was changed to observe the Sabbath, and golf in general would follow.

I lay it squarely in the lap of those who should carry the banner of the Lord, the clergy who are supposed to be his earthly angels in the keeping of the faith. It is they who primarily are at fault and, if they fail, what is to be done?

Once again it will drum at my ears that I am a religious fanatic. I am only an ordinary man, although a
watchman of the coast, if you will. It is the clergy
who are the messengers of God, and why they should
shun their duty is beyond me. They cannot but win in
such a test of their power.

Because, as it says in II Chronicles 36:16:

"But they mocked the messengers of God, and de-
spised his words, and misused his prophets, until the
wrath of the Lord arose against his people, till there
was no remedy."

A sermon for the inmates in the chapel of the South Carolina State Penitentiary, 1964.

The Lord is my shepherd; I shall not want.
Psalms 23:1

In Conclusion

I have told my story as simply as possible.

In summing up the story of Johnny Spence, sinner—never to be a saint—all that I can say in ending it is that, having been saved as I walked through the valley of the shadow of death, I will go anywhere, anytime, to help others of my fellow men find their way to God.

With a prayer of infinite gratitude, I can only add one last verse, Ecclesiastes 7:8, which in my case, at least, is without contradiction:

"Better is the end of a thing than the beginning thereof."

The Authors and Their Book

JOHNNY SPENCE *was born June 20, 1912, in Columbia, South Carolina. He played his first game of golf at the age of ten on a two-hole course in his back yard. At fifteen, he was a finalist in the Columbia City golf championship, and at seventeen was the professional at the Ridgewood Country Club, one of the largest in the Southeast. After serving in the Army during World War II, Spence joined the Professional Golf Association circuit, which he followed for ten years. During this period, he originated the open-air golf shops, which have since been used at all of the major golf championships in the country. He has had wide experience in radio and television and has produced many shows in connection with his golf activities. In 1958, Johnny Spence experienced a religious conversion and, since that time, has traveled throughout the United States doing God's work.*

OSCAR FRALEY, *national sports columnist, is author of the Bill Stern story,* A Taste of Ashes *(Holt, 1959), and the Judge Crater story,* The Empty Robe *(Doubleday, 1961). He is co-author of books on many subjects from cooking to the F.B.I. One of these latter books,* The Untouchables *(Messner, 1957), written with Eliot Ness, became a popular television series. The adventures of Eliot Ness were continued in* Four Against the Mob *(Popular Library, 1961), and later in* The Last of The Untouchables *(Popular Library, 1962), written with Paul Robsky. His two most recent collaborations are* My Wonderful World of Golf *with Toney Penna (Centaur House, 1965) and* The All-Star Athletes Cook Book *(Centaur House, 1965).*

A CENTAUR HOUSE BOOK